blogging for
creatives

Robin Houghton

blogging for creatives

How designers, artists, crafters
and writers can blog to make
contacts, win business
and build success

BLOGGING FOR CREATIVES

First published in the United Kingdom in 2012 by
ILEX
210 High Street
Lewes
East Sussex
BN7 2NS

Copyright © 2012 The Ilex Press Limited

Publisher: Alastair Campbell
Creative Director: James Hollywell
Managing Editor: Nick Jones
Senior Editor: Ellie Wilson
Commissioning Editors: Nadine Monem
& Emma Shackleton
Art Director: Julie Weir
Designer: Simon Goggin

British Library Cataloguing-in-Publication Data
A catalogue record for this book is available
from the British Library.

ISBN: 978-1-908150-26-4

Printed and bound in China

Colour Origination by Ivy Press Reprographics

10 9 8 7 6 5 4 3

CONTENTS

INTRODUCTION

Congratulations! If you want to know about blogging, this book will get you started on what could become a lifelong hobby or enterprise.

Why write a book about blogging? Don't people just Google "how to start blogging" and go from there?

It is true, there is a huge amount of information on the web about blogging. There are blog gurus, blog tutorials, veteran bloggers, expert commentators . . . you could spend all day, every day reading about how to blog. For several years. And still feel that there is more to learn.

That's the problem with learning from web sources —yes, it can be done, but who has the time to sift through it all? How do you decide what's relevant or authoritative? If you read two conflicting pieces of advice, which do you believe? At what point can you say "now I know how to blog"?

You will probably never feel you know everything about blogging, but in this book I aim to give you as much of the nuts and bolts, insights, and inspiration as I can to get you started.

Part of the fun of having a blog is the process of building and maintaining your blog—this will involve learning and discovering as you go along. Trust me, if you've chosen the right topic and understand the basics, it won't feel like a chore.

My own blogging journey started back in 1997, when I first really discovered the internet. Just for fun, I joined a historic-themed online community and soon found myself customizing my homepage, creating

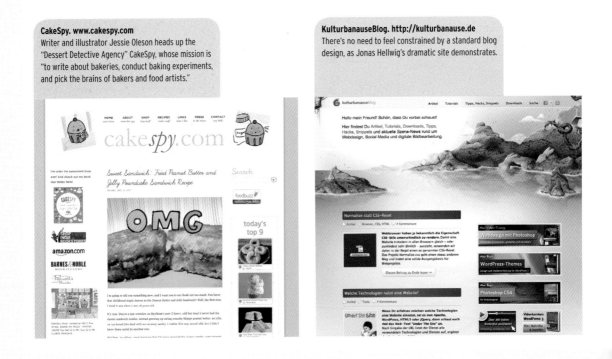

CakeSpy. www.cakespy.com
Writer and illustrator Jessie Oleson heads up the "Dessert Detective Agency" CakeSpy, whose mission is "to write about bakeries, conduct baking experiments, and pick the brains of bakers and food artists."

KulturbanauseBlog. http://kulturbanause.de
There's no need to feel constrained by a standard blog design, as Jonas Hellwig's dramatic site demonstrates.

banners for other members, and contributing to collaborative games and writing projects. I learned HTML (the basic markup code of web pages) and Adobe Photoshop skills. I experimented and made plenty of mistakes, but I also made friends with other community members through sharing, helping, and competing. I learned how to win and lose friends online, about behavior and etiquette, about acronyms, and web-speak.

With hindsight, what started out as a bit of fun was actually an amazing grounding for me as the web developed into what we now recognize as the "social web"–dominated by social networking, blogging, and sharing the stuff we enjoy.

By the time blogging came around I'd found my niche in online marketing, so that's what I started blogging about, and still do. (With forays into poetry and costuming along the way!)

Technology moves on very quickly, and blogging technology is no exception to the rule. By the time you read this there will no doubt be new blogging and micro-blogging platforms, some companies will have gone bust and others bought out, and new trends will be vying for our attention.

But the thing to remember is that blogging is basically about people–people who, like you, want to express their creativity, showcase their work with those who are interested, generate new interests in people, talk about what they love, and learn from others. The technology allows us to do this, so let's go get the best out of it!

Robin Houghton

EXPERT TIP: GRACE BONNEY

Blog: Design*Sponge

http://www.designsponge.com

Started: 2004

Topic: Design

"When I started Design*Sponge it was really about finding a release for all the energy and excitement I had about design. The web seemed like a good place to give voice to that passion, and I feel really lucky to have found a community of people who felt the same way.

"I would say the project has sort of become my life. These days I'm trying to focus more on knowing when to put down my work and pick up my outside life, because it's easy to completely disappear into your work when it doesn't feel like work. But I wouldn't change it for the world."

Credentials: Design*Sponge is a design blog run by Brooklyn-based writer Grace Bonney. The blog currently has 75,000 daily readers on the main site, over 120,000 RSS readers, 280,000 plus Twitter followers, and 20,000 Facebook followers. Grace has been a featured guest on Good Morning America, The Nate Berkus Show, and The Martha Stewart Show, and has been a keynote speaker for a wide variety of organizations and national corporations.

CHAPTER ONE:
GETTING STARTED

WHAT IS A BLOG?

A blog (a shortened form of the word "weblog") is a particular type of website, consisting of articles (or posts) usually time-stamped, and organized in reverse chronology so that the visitor always sees the most recent post first.

In a nutshell, each time you blog, this is essentially what you do:

1. *Log on to the admin pages of your blog.*
2. *Write your post and upload whatever content you like.*
3. *Press the publish button.*

Instantly, your words and images appear on your blog, automatically formatted and added to previous posts with the layout and style that you've set up.

Of course there's bit more to it than that, but once you're all set up, that is basically it. Not too scary, is it?

Blogging has been around in one shape or form since the late 1990s, but really took off around the mid-2000s. The first blogs were kind of internet filters, set up by people who wanted to pass on interesting information they had found on the net, often with their own commentary attached. Bloggers were rather like editors or researchers.

Many blogs still follow this formula, although a growing number are more about expressing and showcasing thoughts, ideas, and creative work, rather than purely commenting on that of others. It's this kind of creative-minded blogger that this book is designed to

Cake with Giants.
http://cakewithgiants.com
This wonderfully clean and quirky blog is one of three run by Australian illustrator and designer Amy Borrell. The pale colors and uncluttered look are the perfect backdrop to Amy's illustrations and photos.

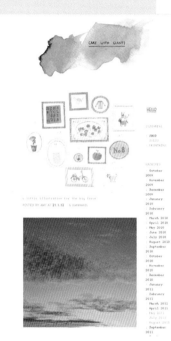

help. Your blog might be an online journal or a showcase for what you're working on, but you will probably also be sharing and talking about things that interest you and other people's work that you love.

Evan Williams is perhaps best known for being one of the founders of Twitter, but years before that he was involved in another blog platform, Blogger. In an interview in 2001 he said this: "To me, the blog concept is about three things: Frequency, Brevity, and Personality." This is still good advice, and in this book, through examples and expert tips, I'll show you what it means.

GET FAMILIAR WITH THE BASIC ELEMENTS OF A BLOG

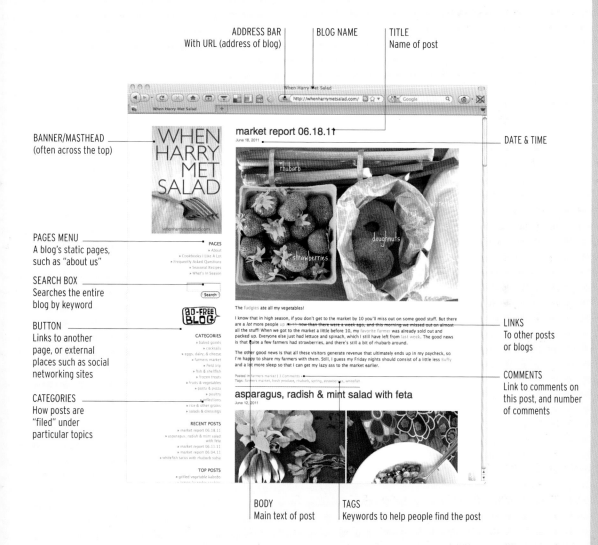

ADDRESS BAR
With URL (address of blog)

BLOG NAME

TITLE
Name of post

BANNER/MASTHEAD
(often across the top)

DATE & TIME

PAGES MENU
A blog's static pages,
such as "about us"

SEARCH BOX
Searches the entire
blog by keyword

BUTTON
Links to another
page, or external
places such as social
networking sites

LINKS
To other posts
or blogs

COMMENTS
Link to comments on
this post, and number
of comments

CATEGORIES
How posts are
"filed" under
particular topics

BODY
Main text of post

TAGS
Keywords to help people find the post

FINDING YOUR NICHE

Jay Mug. http://www.jaymug.com
Jay Mug is the personal blog of an entrepreneur/
marketing professional from the Netherlands and
Hong Kong, which he describes as "a mash up of
everything I like, see, and want to share with you."

Lunch Bag Art. http://lunchbagart.tumblr.com
Focusing on a very specific niche is one way of standing
out and can win you a very loyal audience, as is the
case with Lunch Bag Art.

There are so many blogs out there, but YOURS is going
to be one of the best! OK, it's great to have ambition,
but how do you turn it into reality?

Firstly, you need real passion for the subject of
your blog. It's going to be something that you wake up
in the night thinking about, and when you get out of
bed in the morning you can't wait to blog about it. It's
something that gets you talking animatedly, even to
strangers. It's the thing you love so much you can't
figure out why everyone else doesn't feel the same!

It might also be related to how you earn your living,
but then again it might not. Many top blogs are by
amateurs, in the original sense of the word, that is,
people who do something for the love of it, rather than
to get paid. It's a shame that the word amateur is now
associated with "doing a not very good job" because
that's not what it used to mean at all. In fact, blogging
can and does lead to new opportunities and paid work
for some people.

The second thing to think about is how much
competition is out there, and how your blog will be
different enough to catch and maintain people's
attention. Your blog will always be unique, especially if
you inject your personality into it. But that alone may
not be enough to make your blog stand out.

Do some research. Maybe you already know of
some great blogs in your subject area. Perhaps they
are the reason you want to blog yourself—you've been
inspired and have thought, "I could do that!" Visit these
blogs, subscribe to them in a feed reader (if you haven't
already), and check out their blog rolls—lists of related
blogs, often displayed in a sidebar. Chances are, you
will discover many more blogs on the same or similar
subjects. Some blog titles will appear again and again,
and it is likely they are the most popular and influential.

Before long you will be subscribed to a good number
of blogs. What do they do well? What do you like about

TAKE IT FURTHER: BLOG RESEARCH

Researching other blogs isn't just something to do before you start blogging. Finding, subscribing to, and commenting on other blogs will help you build up a rich network of blogging buddies, as well as provide daily inspiration. To find great blogs, as well as checking out blog rolls and blog search engines like Google Blogs and Technorati, also search Facebook and Twitter for your chosen topics. Get yourself a feed reader: Google Reader is free, and combined with Feedly is a great way of keeping up with blogs. Then, when you find a blog you like, hit the "subscribe" option and there you are.

---

them? What would you do differently? Don't worry at this stage about *how* you can do it, just create a kind of wish list of what you think is going to make your blog really different and exciting.

Thirdly, imagine your blog as a separate life form. A vibrant blog is much more than the sum of its parts—content, design, personality—it is a mini-community in itself, within a far larger network. What kind of community do you want to create? What kind of people do you imagine visiting and enjoying your blog? It's going to be up to you to set the tone, manage visitors' expectations, and shape a vision for your blog.

It's a sad fact that the majority of blogs are abandoned within three months, usually because people lose heart and lack a proper plan. But if you can identify your passion, know how your blog will be different from all the rest, and have a vision for its future, then you have a better than average chance of long-term success.

The Technorati Top 100

WHAT TYPE OF BLOGGER ARE YOU?

Darling Clementine. http://dcstudio.tumblr.com
Norwegian designers and illustrators Ingrid Reithaug
and Tonje Holand have a Tumblr blog as a companion
to their main business website.

Even before you start blogging it's worth thinking for a
moment about the type of blogger you're going to be.
Your motivations for blogging, and the style of blog that
suits your creative type, will go a long way in determining
the type of blog you may want to create.

It's all about motivation . . .

Why do you want to blog? Is it to tell the world about
something you feel passionately about? To offer helpful
tips? To build your personal "brand?" To make money?
To promote your business?

Here are the most common blog types. You may recognize
yourself as being in one category, or overlapping more
than one.

Hobby Blogger: Do you have a burning interest in
something specific—photography, family trees, cookery,
anime, parenting . . . ? Hobby bloggers are enthusiasts
who love nothing better than to share and discuss with
other like-minded individuals. Be careful though: it can
be addictive, and for some hobby bloggers it turns into
a career.

Authority Blogger: Are you an expert with knowledge
to share? In the blogosphere, "authority" status doesn't
come instantly, but if you are committed to staying at
the forefront of your subject area, enjoy educating and
informing others, and want to enhance your reputation
or that of your company, then this may be you.

The Elegant Variation.
http://marksarvas.blogs.com/elegvar
Mark Sarvas's literary blog is where he interviews
writers, reviews books, and shares what he's working on
with his students. The blog has won numerous awards.

Pro Blogger: As it sounds, this type of blogger
approaches it as a business. If you are looking to make
money from your blogging, you are up against some
tough competition—but that's not to say it can't be
done! If you fall into this category, you're likely to have
a thick skin and a willingness to work hard.

Journal Blogger: Do you just want to share your life's experiences with the world? Journal bloggers write about their lives—family, pets, travels, work, and the like. They blog simply for the fun of sharing and expressing themselves.

. . . and creative type!

Do you enjoy writing? Then you'll be happy writing blog posts. But blogging doesn't have to be about the written word.

Other people are more visual—they are inspired by images, photos, diagrams, video, and are better able to express themselves through visual media.

Or are you more of a speaker and listener? Aural types may be more at home producing an audio blog or regular podcasts.

The better you understand your blogger type the easier it will be to make the right choices in the setting up and planning stages. This, in turn, will increase your chances of building and sustaining a successful blog.

EXPERT TIP: GLENNA HARRIS

Blog: Knitting to Stay Sane
http://crazyknittinglady.wordpress.com
Started: 2006
Topic: Knitting

"Why do I blog? I knit. I like to knit. I like to talk about knitting. The blog is a way to extend this to a wider group of people. And sure, there are the occasional non-knitting posts like, say, when I run a half-marathon and want to tell you about it. (But honestly, if I do something like run a half-marathon, I'm telling everyone I know.) I write posts on my little laptop and submit them to the internet, and if I'm lucky, other people will read them, and if I'm very lucky, other people will read them and find them meaningful in some way."

Credentials: Canadian blogger Glenna got truly serious about knitting while studying for her PhD, as a form of stress relief and distraction. Since then she has added knitting design and teaching to her repertoire. Her patterns have been featured in *Canadian Living Magazine*, *Knitty*, and *Magknits*, and online through Ravelry and Patternfish. Knitting to Stay Sane is hosted at WordPress.com.

BLOGGING WITH OTHERS

If the thought of blogging is a little daunting or you're worried you may not always find the time, there are ways to lighten the load.

For example, how about getting together with a friend and starting a blog in partnership with them? Or perhaps you're part of a ready-made group—people you work alongside in the same studio or building, or people you see regularly at events . . .

Your motivation for co-blogging might be purely to do with pooling your expertise and sharing the responsibility, or perhaps your vision for the blog goes beyond a simple showcase of your own work and ideas.

Either way, blogging with others can be extremely satisfying. Creatives love to collaborate and bounce off each other!

Blogging with a partner/co-blogging

If you're thinking of going into blogging with another person, from the start you'll need to both be honest with each other: are you both equally committed to the project? Do you want the same things, or at least mutually acceptable things for the blog? Are either of you the kind of person who loses interest in things or is more of a "starter" than a "finisher?"

Cupcakes Take the Cake.
http://www.cupcakestakethecake.blogspot.com
Friends Rachel Kramer Bussel, Nichelle Stephens, and Stacie Joy started their blog in 2004 and made NBC News in 2008. They have four "cupcake correspondents."

Cairo. http://cairocollection.blogspot.com
Joel Leshefka and Justine Ashbee run Cairo, a Seattle store selling vintage housewares and clothing. Their blog is as eclectic as the store and features interviews, impromptu photoshoots, audio tracks, and a lot more.

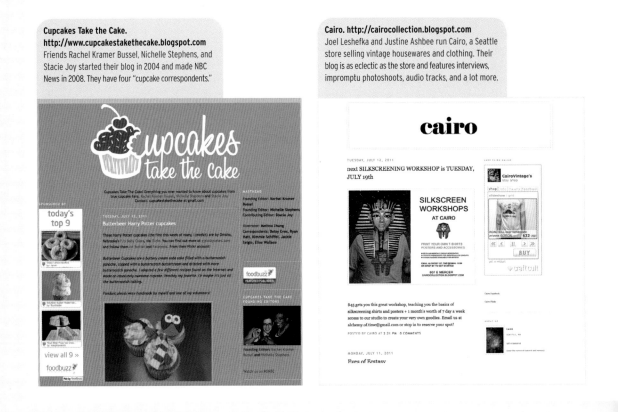

It may sound harsh, but it's only fair that you both think about your answers to these questions now. If one person ends up doing more work than the other it can lead to resentment. If you're both doing this for fun, rather than business, you may find this kind of advice a little heavy. But given the time and effort you're about to invest, it's worth it!

Benefits: If all partners agree how the workload is to be shared (and then stick to it) this is a great solution for those without the time to post regularly and frequently. Two heads are better than one when it comes to generating good content ideas, and when one person may be feeling uninspired the other can step in. If you have complementary skills, for example one person has some technical know-how and the other is great at promotion, even better.

Downsides: As with any partnership, mutual trust and a shared vision is important. Also, be aware that you may have very different styles. This may lead to a variety of content on your blog, but readers will appreciate some elements of consistency also. Both parties must be willing to give and take.

Hipsterfood. http://hipsterfood.tumblr.com
Hipsterfood is a blog "to show you that vegan food isn't just for hipsters!" It's run by Bob and Cara, who in 2011 launched a companion quarterly magazine, *Chickpea*, that's produced in print form and can also be read online.

GROUP BLOGGING

If you're new to blogging, or have been blogging for a while but still have only a small readership, one way to gain more exposure is to contribute to a group blog. Group (or collective) blogs are showcases for individuals under the umbrella of a particular topic or theme, and generally come in three forms: invitation-only, curated (or edited), and non-curated.

As it sounds, an invitation-only group blog will feature posts by people who have been asked to contribute. Many top blogs are in this format and the bigger ones may have an editorial team. Getting invited onto a large, successful blog may seem an unattainable goal, but even the humblest blogger, if he or she has something unusual or unique to offer, can catch an editor's eye.

A curated site will have one or more gatekeepers: people you need to impress with your content in order to get published on the blog. There will be certain standards and criteria for inclusion and you have to submit your posts and hope for the best.

Contributing to a group blog

Benefits: Curated sites can have large and potentially influential audiences so your work may appear alongside that of others you admire. You may get the opportunity to be a featured contributor, or even get discovered as a new talent. If you struggle to get onto curated blogs you could start by contributing to a non-curated site.

Downsides: As is true of much of the edited media, getting exposure on a curated blog can be quite competitive. On the other hand, if a site lets anyone post then the overall standard may not be high, so consider whether you want your work to appear there.

Taste Spotting. http://www.tastespotting.com
Taste Spotting is a "visual potluck of recipes, references, experiences, stories, articles, products, and anything else that inspires exquisite taste." The blog welcomes contributions and is edited by Jennifer Bartoli.

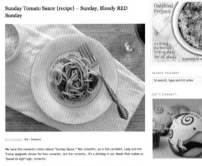

Light Stalking. http://www.lightstalking.com
Edited by Rob Wood, Light Stalking is a group blog about beautiful photography and "putting great photographers in front of the audience they deserve."

Creating a group blog

Do you see an opportunity to start a group blog? There is nothing to stop you! If you are known in your field, are good at developing contacts and publicity, and love the work of others and the idea of sharing that love, this could be for you. It doesn't have to be defined by genre either—plenty of successful blogs are basically personal collections of somebody's favorite things.

Benefits: You get to pick and choose from other people's great content and there's less pressure on you to come up with original content all the time. You can showcase your work alongside that of people you admire and are inspired by.

Downsides: You need to make your blog a desirable place to be seen, in order to attract some great contributions. Some people may only be interested in taking part if you can show you have a large, good-quality audience, and that takes resources and effort to build up.

Lovely Stationery. http://lovelystationery.com
Lovely Stationery reaches over 5,000 people daily from over 150 countries. It's a curated blog, meaning anyone can submit work but only the best are showcased.

EXPERT TIP: RICKY SALSBERRY

Blog: The Donut Project
http://www.thedonutproject.com
Started: 2009
Topic: Design

"In my opinion, I think people make the best content when they're writing/posting about something they truly care about. There are times on our blog where we make five posts a day, and other times we don't post for two weeks. We do this because we don't want to post something just to post something. That goes against most advice you'll hear on how to build a consistent readership, but we simply don't care. We won't feed bad content to our audience just to hit an imaginary schedule."

Credentials: The Donut Project is a design inspiration site created by a group of young designers who "aspire to inspire." The blog focuses on content that's not strictly to do with graphic design, but is definitely thought-provoking. As they say on the blog, "the design world needs to read more than the same award annuals and list posts, and we hope to be part of the good stuff."

INTRODUCING THE BLOGOSPHERE

You are about to enter an alien zone! A world that brings out both the best and the worst in people, a haven for citizen journalists and creative souls alike; an Aladdin's cave of ephemera with something for everyone. Yes folks, welcome to the Blogosphere.

The practice of blogging is fundamentally a 21st-century phenomenon. The first bloggers were techies. They had to be, because in 1999 there was nothing quite like the content management systems of today. Blogging only really took off with the advent of blogging software, making it easy, accessible, and free. The first wave of non-techie bloggers were conspiracy theorists, political commentators, and news pundits. The hyperlinks between one blog and another meant that ideas could fly round the internet and opinions could spread at an amazing pace.

Even now, that's why brands and organizations spend huge resources identifying and wooing influential bloggers—those whose audience and credibility means that a positive opinion expressed on their blog can have an immediate effect on sales and action.

Nowadays, anybody with access to the internet and nothing more than a smartphone can start a blog or micro-blog, which is both a good and a bad thing!

As the blogosphere grows, more and more blogs are competing for people's attention, and it's inevitable that some blogs just will not survive. A blog needs to be connected to other blogs, it needs constant nurturing, and above all it needs an audience. This is true even if your blog is to be simply an online journal.

Despite the rise of social networking, which some predicted would make blogging redundant, the blogosphere is as healthy today as ever. If anything, sites like Facebook and LinkedIn have introduced even more people to the idea of what marketers call "user-generated content"—which is, in other words, posting your own photos, video, commentary, and creative material—and this in turn has fueled a new generation of would-be bloggers.

The number of blogs has grown from a handful in 1999 to an estimated 100 million plus today. Even in 2005, there were an estimated 15,000 blogs being created every single day. According to Technorati, just about half the world's bloggers are in the US, 65

Easy Makes Me Happy.
http://easymakesmehappy.blogspot.com
A focal point of Tara Murray's workspace is the yarn rack made by her husband and wall-mounted above her desk. Tara blogs about crochet, crafts, and design.

percent of bloggers are hobbyists, and 21 percent are self-employed or small business owners.

So are there just too many blogs? In a 2010 interview with Technorati, Lisa Stone, co-founder and CEO of BlogHer, Inc. said: "It's a bit like asking are there too many movies. No, I don't think there are too many blogs–I'm not sure there are enough good ones!"

TAKE IT FURTHER: TECHNORATI

Blog search engine and directory Technorati.com was founded in 2002 to help promote blogs and blogging. It publishes an annual "State of the Blogosphere" report and a "Top 100" list of blogs that's updated daily. Technorati is a great resource for finding interesting blogs and blog posts as well as a valuable mine of information about blogging.

EXPERT TIP: AMY NG

Blog: Pikaland: The Illustrated Life

http://pikaland.com

Started: 2008

Topic: Illustration and design

"Be careful of burnout when you're starting a blog–lots of people start up quickly, throwing on lots of content and working hard around the clock to maintain it. But in your rush to start, always remember to pace yourself. Blogging is a slow jog, not a short sprint!"

Credentials: Amy Ng was an editor at a regional architecture and design magazine before realizing that her first love was illustration. Pikaland is a blog about living the illustrated life–a collection of inspirations and beautiful things made/designed by illustrators and artists, updated almost daily.

CHAPTER TWO:
BLOGGING TOOLS AND TECHNOLOGY

HOW TO CHOOSE A BLOGGING PLATFORM

Do you need to be tech-savvy to set up a blog? Not necessarily—as you will see in this chapter. But you will need to engage with the technology a little, even if just at the beginning, as the choices you make at this stage will affect what you can do with your blog further down the line.

Most new bloggers choose one of a handful of popular blogging platforms (sometimes called blogware or blogging software providers), because they are easy to use and free. I will be focusing on three of them in the next chapter.

However, before making that choice, it's worth thinking about your plans for the blog. For example:

- *Are you going to be blogging for fun, or is it to support a business or professional interest?*
- *Will you be posting a large number of photos, video, or other content on your blog?*
- *Do you want to sell advertising space on your blog, or make money from it?*
- *How quickly do you see the blog growing, and are you planning to attract large numbers of visitors?*
- *Do you mainly want to blog on the move, from a phone or other mobile device?*
- *Will there be more than one contributor or blog administrator?*

Allsorts.
http://allsorts.typepad.com
Allsorts is the blog of illustrator and designer Jenny B Harris, where she shares ideas and inspirations, patterns, freebies, and more. It's hosted at Typepad.

Some blogging platforms will be more suitable than others—take a look at the kinds of blogs they host and read the small print before committing to anything.

Hosted options: free or almost free

Many of today's bloggers, even the most experienced and successful, started small with a free or low-cost hosted blog, often using a ready-made template or theme. A provider such as Blogger.com or WordPress.com will set you up with space for your blog, the tools to manage it via a web interface or a mobile application, and plenty of pre-designed templates.

The platform you choose will generally determine where your blog is hosted. For example, if you sign up for Blogger then your blog will sit on Blogger servers and will be called "yourname.blogspot.com." If you are not keen on the idea of having the host name as part of your blog's address, you can still have your own domain name for your blog (see p. 22, Take it Further).

Some blog hosting is low-cost rather than free, for example, Typepad. Nevertheless we are only talking about a few dollars a month for the basic level. All providers have more than one level of service, usually depending upon how much content you will be uploading each month, how much customization you need, whether you want to be able to create more than one blog, or install special features.

Even if you have big ambitions for your blog, there is a lot to be said for starting this way. You can learn about blogging, make mistakes, and experiment, without any outlay other than your time. You may or may not outgrow your chosen platform, but remember, all blogging platforms have their own proprietary systems, which you will learn how to use and become familiar with. Changing to another will involve a certain amount of starting over.

MORE HOSTING OPTIONS

Hello hello! http://hellohellodesign.tumblr.com
This blog by a New York graphic designer/illustrator looks quite different on a mobile phone to the computer screen.

Hosted, micro blog

The popularity of micro-blogging has really grown over the last few years, so much so that many high profile bloggers now also run a micro-blog in parallel.

Micro-blogging platforms include Tumblr, TypePad Micro, and Posterous, and they are designed to make it as easy as possible to post or share while on the move or away from your computer. They have inbuilt tools to allow people to share your blog posts with their friends on social networks and within the micro-blogging community—great if your aim is to post brief, timely updates to your blog and have them shared around the social web. These micro platforms are particularly popular with photo and video bloggers.

Self-hosted

As an alternative to a hosted blog, there are providers that allow you to download and install blogging software on your own domain space, either for free or for a licence fee. For example, WordPress.com offers a free hosted blog, but at WordPress.org you can download its blogware and do your own thing.

TAKE IT FURTHER: DOMAIN MAPPING

Even if you have a hosted blog you can still make it look like your blog sits on your own domain. You can do this either by creating a URL, for example www.mydomain.com/blog and redirecting it to myblogname.typepad.com, which is quick and easy, but that will only mask the URL in the browser bar. For a more permanent solution, you can enable domain mapping. This will permanently change all the URLs of your blog posts to include your domain rather than the blog host. This is sometimes only available on paid hosting plans.

This is called a self-hosted blog, and it does allow you more freedom and flexibility over functionality and design. It could be a good option if you already have a personal or business website and you want your blog to be hosted on the same domain, or if you're likely to outgrow the themes or templates available on the free blog platforms. And free blogging platforms are not always suitable, for example if you're planning to make money from your blog, or want a unique design or unique features. If you go down this route you will need to have some technical know-how. (Or know someone who does!)

If your blog becomes heavily trafficked or very big, you may need to find a new home for it with dedicated hosting. However, your hosting costs will certainly go up—if you want a blog that functions quickly and effectively then you will have to pay for the extra space and transfer speed.

Book by its Cover.
http://www.book-by-its-cover.com
Powered by WordPress, Book by its Cover is a self-hosted blog with a unique layout and look.

Ellis Nadler's Sketchbook.
http://ellisnadler.blogspot.com
Freelance illustrator, artist, photographer, and author Ellis Nadler has opted for Blogger.

Confessions of a Cookbook Queen.
http://confessionsofacookbookqueen.com
Kristan is a mom living in rural Arkansas. Her blog, using WordPress blogware, focuses on simple recipes and aspects of her daily life and has a strong following of readers.

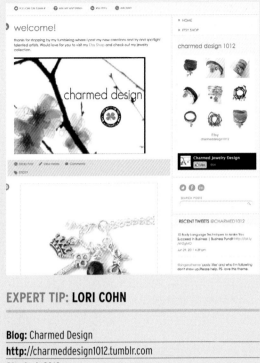

EXPERT TIP: **LORI COHN**

Blog: Charmed Design
http://charmeddesign1012.tumblr.com
Started: 2010
Topic: Jewelry

"The beauty of Tumblr lies in its simplicity and clean, modern design. Themes are numerous, stylish, and easy to customize. Posting is a breeze. There is also a sense of community lacking in other platforms. Users follow each other, liking, and reblogging posts."

Credentials: Lori Cohn is a former lawyer who began making jewelry while recovering from a life-threatening illness. Her jewelry reflects her experience and love for life, and the feeling that she is indeed charmed.

What's your favorite blogging platform?

Bloggers get mightily attached to their chosen blogging software! Here are some of the comments I've had in answer to this question:

I've been using Textpattern for the past five years, and I absolutely love it. I've tried Blogger, WordPress, and a whole lot of other platforms, although admittedly it took me about two months to figure out how everything worked! I must say that their forum and the lovely, close-knit community is really helpful—all the people who answered my questions six years ago are still there, going strong, and still helping everyone out!
Amy Ng, Pikaland (http://pikaland.com)

I started using Blogger because it was very simple to set up and the other platforms at the time seemed a bit daunting. It's never been cutting-edge when it comes to the technical bells and whistles, but they seem to eventually add all of the features I've wanted. I've also appreciated the fact that it's got fairly seamless integration with other Google products that I already use. Sure, they've had some technical problems over the years, but it's hard to complain too much about it considering I've never had to pay a cent for the use of their service. Generally it's been a very easy platform to use and I especially appreciate that they've given me tons of free space for uploading and storing images.
Noah Scalin, Make Something 365 (http://makesomething365.blogspot.com)

I first created my personal blog through Blogger and, when it came to writing my business blog, I looked into WordPress after being persuaded it was a superior platform. But I found Blogger so much easier to use so went with that instead. Although I would like to bring my blog into my (business) WordPress website, part of me is a little reluctant as Google is integrated so much into my working life. **Joanne Munro, Chaos Killer (http://www.chaoskiller.com)**

BLOG LAYOUTS & CONVENTIONS

Many websites are built using blogging software, but that doesn't mean they are blogs. We already established in Chapter 1 what a blog actually is, so how do you recognize one? Are there any hard-and-fast conventions you need to follow? What are the elements of a blog that are common to all, and what makes a blog unique?

Date & time

The first and perhaps most obvious thing that shouts "blog" is when you see a date stamp. The latest blog post will be there on the homepage of the blog, usually with the date and time it was posted. In case of a group blog or one with numerous contributors, it may also name the author of the post. Older posts appear below, in reverse date order.

There are exceptions to this. For example, you may opt to have a static page as your homepage: perhaps one that welcomes visitors and incentivizes them to subscribe, or if you have a feature or promotion you want to give prominence. Generally though, the idea of a blog is to showcase your regular updates so that each time someone visits it looks different and vibrant.

Exhero. http://exhero.de
Alexander Kaiser's WordPress blog, Exhero, displays short blog extracts on the homepage with the date and number of comments prominent at the side of each.

Papel Continuo. http://www.papelcontinuo.net
The witty design of blog Papel Continuo demonstrates that a three-column WordPress theme needn't being boring.

NEED TO KNOW: REMEMBER TO HIT "SAVE"

Here's a tip that will SAVE you time and energy, but is very easy to forget. Whenever you change a setting, or write a post, make sure you save it. This may sound really basic, but I'd rather not tell you how many times I have changed a set of colors, uploaded something new, or been through a whole page of preferences only to forget to scroll down and hit the SAVE button. The same goes for blog posts. Although you are usually prompted to save, if you're writing long blog posts it might be a good idea to write them offline and paste them into your editor screen.

Masthead

Across the top of the page is usually a masthead featuring the name of the blog and often a short description. Most bloggers are interested in getting people not only to read their blog but to subscribe to it, so the clearer it is for people to see what it's about, the sooner they will decide whether or not to subscribe.

Somewhere below the masthead is generally a menu of the static pages on the site, such as "about us" and "contact." This is often where you see a "subscribe" button. It's a convention of website design that you get all the important things high on the page. People often miss the stuff further down, especially if it involves scrolling.

Body

Typical blog layouts are in columns—one wide and one or two narrow, for example. The wider column is where the body of the blog posts appear, while the narrow columns (or sidebars as they are known) tend to contain various material, from lists of related blogs (blogrolls) and previous posts to adverts, buttons, and other static items.

You will notice that micro-blogs are often narrower and may not have the conventional layout—there may be no masthead, or the menu may be smaller or even non-existent. Take a look at the Tumblr blogs on these pages, for example. Micro-blogs tend to be optimized for display on mobile devices where too many menus or too much width can detract from the main body of the post, especially if it is a photo or video.

Aidosaur. http://aidosaur.tumblr.com
NYC-based cartoonist Yuko blogs at aidosaur.tumblr. com. One narrow column is ideal for viewing on a mobile device.

Just Monk3y. http://monk3y.tumblr.com
Matt Taylor says his Tumblelog is a "digital sketchbook of my mind's interior."

COMMENTS, PLUGINS, & WIDGETS

Comments

A blog isn't usually just a one-way conversation. One of the most exciting and defining features of your blog will be the ability for people to comment. A vibrant, well-established blog may attract many comments, but don't be disheartened if it takes some time for yours to do so. That is very typical and it doesn't necessarily mean nobody is reading the blog. Nurture your commenters—thank people for taking the time and keep the conversation going. As you will find when you comment on other blogs, there's nothing more disheartening than to be ignored after you've taken the time to comment!

There are many ways of attracting comments, starting with the type of content you are posting. (See Chapter 5 for more on this.) On the other hand, you will want to manage comments, as they will not always be the sort you want on your blog. You will almost certainly encounter "comment spam"—meaningless or irrelevant comments by anonymous posters. Much of it is automated, carried out by spam bots, but thankfully there are things you can do to prevent it, such as installing a plugin like Akismet (see p. 28, Need to Know) and adjusting your blog settings.

Plugins

When you set up your blog, although it may seem you have everything you need for it, it's amazing how quickly you start thinking "wouldn't it be good if I could do/have this." You probably can—what you need is the relevant plugin (or plug-in).

Guerilla Embroidery. http://guerilla-embroidery.blogspot.com
Sarah Terry's blog is where she promotes her unique embroidered accessories and artworks, many of which appear in collections all over the world, including the Tate Britain gallery in London.

Embroidery with an Edge

Featuring the art, craft and general mad rantings of Sarah Terry, the artist behind Guerilla Embroidery

MONDAY, 23 MAY 2011

Flickr Response Project: Guerilla Embroidery vs. C-Urchin

ABOUT ME

Guerilla Embroidery
Todmorden, United Kingdom

In 2004, I was long listed for the Hand&Lock Hand embroidery prize. I graduated in 2006 with a degree in Embroidery from the Manchester Metropolitan University. In 2007, I set up my business 'Guerilla Embroidery' and have been making unique embroidered accessories and artworks for sale since then. My work is in collections all over the world, including the USA, Australia and Europe, and the Tate Britain. I am available for bespoke embroidery work, workshops and commissions. Please do not hesitate to contact me.

View my complete profile

EXPERT TIP: NOAH SCALIN

Blog: Skull-A-Day

http://skulladay.blogspot.com

Started: 2007

Topic: A project to make and showcase a skull a day

"Definitely pay attention to your readers. A great deal of the success of Skull-A-Day was based on the fact that I let the fans dictate the content of the site as well as reaching out to them for the feedback. The site is now almost entirely populated with reader submissions and run by three volunteers who were previously regular commenters on the site."

Credentials: Noah Scalin's project in 2007–2008 was to make a skull a day for a year, and in year two it consisted of daily submissions by readers. Since then it has continued to thrive, always on the theme of skulls, and Noah's book *Skulls*, published by Lark Books, featured 150 of the original pieces.

Plugins are small items of software that can add something extra to your blog's existing capability. Some are platform-specific, but many work across blogging platforms. New plugins and updates are being developed all the time; always make sure your version is up-to-date.

The most popular plugins (as opposed to widgets) are those which help improve a blog's security, analytics, promotion, and comment handling. There are thousands of them—just search for the issue you are trying to solve and you will probably find a plugin for it.

On a hosted blog you will be able to choose from plugins and widgets provided by your platform provider, and because your blog sits on their servers it usually means these little extras are pre-installed and often pre-activated, so you don't need to do anything.

However, if you are self-hosting your blog you will be responsible for sourcing and installing plugins, making sure the software is up to date, and that you have taken the necessary security measures to keep your blog safe from hackers.

Need to know: plugins vs. widgets

Plugins sometimes work completely in the background, while others are visible on your blog—but those are generally known as widgets. A widget has a nice graphical interface and looks good in a blog's sidebar. Basically what you *see* is the widget, but what it *does* is the plugin behind it.

NEED TO KNOW: COMMENT SPAM

The purpose of comment spam is to create links back to the spammer's site and artificially raise its search ranking. It is possible to stop the majority of comment spam, but it involves a balance between keeping spammers out and making it easy for legitimate people to comment.

ALL ABOUT WIDGETS

Here's where you can really accessorize your blog! Widgets (or in Blogger, "gadgets") are the visual representation of a plugin, that is, they are small bits of software that add some extra functionality to your blog. You can generally customize the color scheme, size, fonts, and many other aspects of a widget. In a classic two- or three-column blog layout, widgets generally display in the sidebar.

There are a number of standard sidebar widgets that are common to most blogging platforms. When setting up your blog you can decide which ones you want to activate and display. These include things like a blog post Archive, Blog Roll (list of blogs you want to link to), and Recent Posts.

Each individual blog platform then has its own pre-installed widgets, often with proprietary names. For example, TypePad has things called TypeLists, which can be used to display text, links, buttons, images, or whatever you wish. WordPress, in particular, is famous for its huge number and range of widgets and plugins.

When browsing blogs that you admire, take note of any interesting, unusual, or fun widgets or buttons you could install on your blog. Be careful to think of your visitors, who may enjoy "fun stuff" but might be turned off if the page starts to get too cluttered! Here are a few examples of what you could add, simply by installing and customizing the relevant widget:

- *Share, like, and rate buttons*
- *Newsletter subscribe forms*
- *Polls and games*
- *Slideshows, tag clouds*
- *Twitter feeds*
- *Site search*
- *Adverts (if your host allows)*
  . . . and much more.

Joe McNally Photography.
http://www.joemcnally.com/blog
Photographer Joe McNally has used a custom WordPress theme to give the widgets on his sidebar a unique look.

10 POPULAR WIDGETS

There are thousands of widgets on every conceivable subject. Just searching for "YouTube blog widget" brings up over 6,500 results! This is a selection of some of the most popular, to whet your appetite.

Meebo.
http://www.meebome.com
A nice widget for Blogger users: have a chat window on your blog.

Skype. http://www.skype.com
/intl/en/tell-a-friend/get-a-skype-button
If you're a Skype user, this button makes it easy for people to contact you and see if you're in or out.

Twitter.
http://twitter.com/about/resources/widgets
Display a rolling feed of your own tweets, tweets based on a search term, or any of your lists.

Tag Cloud. http://www.tagcloud-generator.com
Just put in your blog address, customize the look, and generate a tag cloud for your sidebar. The bigger the word, the more times you've blogged on that topic.

Facebook Like Button. https://developers. facebook.com/docs/reference/plugins/like
A "Like" button is one of several ways to integrate your blog with Facebook (see Chapter 8).

**Flickr Badge.
http://www.flickr.com/badge.gne**
Displays photos from a Flickr photostream.

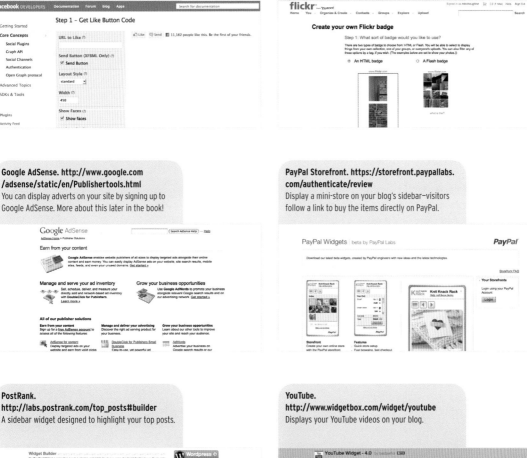

Google AdSense. http://www.google.com /adsense/static/en/Publishertools.html
You can display adverts on your site by signing up to Google AdSense. More about this later in the book!

PayPal Storefront. https://storefront.paypallabs. com/authenticate/review
Display a mini-store on your blog's sidebar–visitors follow a link to buy the items directly on PayPal.

**PostRank.
http://labs.postrank.com/top_posts#builder**
A sidebar widget designed to highlight your top posts.

**YouTube.
http://www.widgetbox.com/widget/youtube**
Displays your YouTube videos on your blog.

WHAT'S IN A NAME?

I'm sure this is something you've already thought about, but let's go through it in more detail—what are you going to call your blog? Take your time—it's not easy to change once your blog is established.

If you already have a business name, or are known professionally by your own name, you may have decided to use that. But if you're a hobby blogger or starting from scratch, choosing a name can be quite momentous! First, ask yourself a few questions:

- *It sounds obvious, but has the name been used already—for example, either for the same type of blog, or a topic you'd rather not be associated with? Do some searches and check.*
- *Do you want it to create a particular impression? For example, professional, playful, indie/alternative, witty, elegant, and so on.*
- *Do you want something descriptive, or abstract? Calling your blog "Knitting Blog" might not be very imaginative but it does at least tell people what it's about, rather than making them have to guess (and potentially guess incorrectly).*
- *Who's your audience? As always, consider who you want to attract and the kind of name that they will remember, or perhaps make them smile.*

At this stage, check if the domain name for your chosen blog name has been registered. Even if you're not fussed about having your own dot com address, you should find out if it clashes with another site. If the domain name hasn't been registered, and you've definitely decided that's the name for you, you should think about buying it. It's not expensive and at some point you may decide to use it for your blog, even if not right away.

Modish.
http://www.modishblog.com/modish
Modish is all about blogger Jena Coray's personal inspirations, style muses, and favorite handmade and vintage goods.

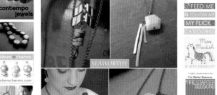

Katie Green Bean.
http://www.katiegreenbean.blogspot.com
The name of illustrator Katie Green's blog combines her school nickname with her real name. She also carries on the "green bean" motif at various points in the blog design.

OK Great.
http://www.okaygreat.com
A successful creative collaboration, OK Great describes itself as "hell-bent on delivering the best in art, design, and culture."

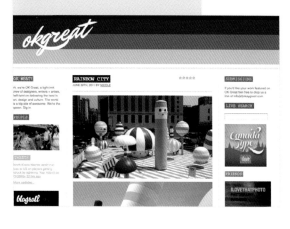

EXPERT TIP: JACKIE CARDY

Blog: DogDaisyChains
http://dogdaisychains.blogspot.com
Started: 2008
Topic: Textiles & Embroidery

"Before you start a blog write a list of several possible names because you can be sure that there will be many others out there with the same idea as you.

I started out on Flickr as Dogdaisy92 . . . yes you've guessed . . . we had a dog called Daisy born in 1992! I thought it would be good to call my blog 'Dogdaisy' but it was taken, as was my second choice 'Daisy Chains.' In a panic because I wanted to get started, I stuck them all together and the result is my slightly nonsensical blog name DogDaisyChains!"

Credentials: Jackie is an embroiderer from a village in Lancashire, England. She works with silk fibers and velvet, and especially loves machine-embroidery. She has exhibited in galleries across England and Ireland.

NEED TO KNOW

Your blog has two names:

1. The name you see in the address bar of your browser (URL)
This is the one that begins http://. This address may appear elsewhere also, for example, sometimes your blog will be referenced from another site using the full http://www.yourblog.com name, or http://yourblog.blogplatform.com if you're using a hosted service and aren't hiding the fact with a redirected URL or domain mapping. (Ouch! If that sounds like gobbledygook turn back to page 22 for a quick reminder of what it means.) Oftentimes the URL will be hidden behind a text link which will simply say <u>Blog name</u> or <u>a great blog about knitting</u> (or whatever your blog's about).

2. The blog's given name
This is the name you'll display on your blog, probably in the masthead or somewhere prominent on the page. The URL usually contains the given name, but in some cases a blogger may prefer for them to be different.

PAGES & POSTS

On the internet there are all kinds of oddities, particularly in the naming of things. We've already seen how widgets are called gadgets in Blogger. One of the first things a newbie blogger needs to understand is the difference between pages and posts.

Posts

- *A post is date- and time-stamped, and it's what you will be creating each time you add to your blog. It is the life and soul of your blog.*
- *A post may consist of text, photos, video, audio . . . any kind of content.*
- *A post will have its own unique web address, or URL, so that it can be linked to directly.*
- *On a blog, older posts are usually archived by month (in the current year) and by year before that.*
- *You can tag or label blog posts with words and phrases to help people find them, and you can put them into categories. (Blogger does not have Categories—see Chapter 3 for more about this).*

Pages

- *A page on a blog is static—it stays in place for the life of your blog and doesn't appear in the stream of posts.*
- *A typical page would be your "About" page, where you can introduce yourself and any other contributors, tell visitors what the blog is about, explain any house rules, and so forth.*
- *Don't forget to add a "Contact" page if you want readers to get in touch.*

Help people find the good stuff

Depending on how often you post, and how long those posts are, your blog will grow into quite a big website. As with any site, people need to be able to find their way around it quickly and easily. You want them to explore, enjoy, and leave comments.

Think of it like an in-tray or a pile of mail. Every time you add to the pile, things get buried and become harder to find. It's much better to have a filing system of some kind.

The Cool Hunter.
http://www.thecoolhunter.co.uk
The wide ranging subect matter of this blog (beautiful discoveries from around the world) means it has a large number of categories on the left-hand sidebar. In addition, the top half of the homepage carries thumbnails to the current "hot picks," keeping the blog fresh and directing visitors to the latest material.

Blogging software offers a range of functions that help you file your blog content so that it can be found easily even if it was posted years ago. On websites, pointers to help you find your way around are often referred to as "navigation," for example, menus that contain links to the pages on the site, using helpful words as pointers.

On a blog, your static pages (About, Contact, and so on) will appear on a menu, just like you would expect to see on any website.

A blog may also have a search box, which allows you search the blog by keyword—a very useful feature.

But the principal "filing system" of the majority of blog platforms is its Categories. When you create a new post, you have the option of assigning it to one or more category. These are rather like drawers in a filing cabinet, except for the fact that the same blog post can appear in more than one simultaneously. (Instead of Categories, Blogger has a system called Labels, which is a cross between tags and categories.)

When a reader sees the categories listed on your blog, he or she can find the subject they're particularly interested in, click on it, and a list of all related blog posts will appear.

When naming categories, think carefully about the words that best describe the content from the visitors' point of view. You can create as many categories as you like, but a smaller number will be easier for the visitor to navigate and less overwhelming.

EXPERT TIP: DAVID AIREY

Blog: David Airey
http://www.davidairey.com
Started: 2005
Topic: Design

"Get involved with blogs in your niche. I regularly visit other design blogs and add to the comment thread conversations. It keeps the interaction flowing and helps strengthen the sense of community. Blog authors appreciate genuine comments, too."

Credentials: David Airey is a graphic designer and design author who has worked in the UK and the United States, and is now based in Northern Ireland, where he works with clients from around the globe. For more insights into his blogging journey read his blog post at www.davidairey.com/top-7-blog-mistakes-to-avoid.

"HOW OFTEN SHOULD I POST?"

This is probably the most frequently asked question of all. Without regular posts your blog will be just another static website—or worse, in fact, if your last post was some time ago. And with a blog, there's nowhere to hide—the date of your last post is right there for all to see on the homepage!

A blog that hasn't been updated in ages will look abandoned, and the web is awash with abandoned or semi-abandoned blogs. In the US alone, there are an estimated 35 million blogs in existence, and yet the majority of those have not been updated in six months or more.

If you're serious about starting and maintaining a vibrant blog with a community of readers and commenters, then you need to post as frequently as you are able. A good rule of thumb is at least once a week. The most popular blogs, and the majority of those that you see in this book, are updated more frequently than that. Look around at other blogs on your subject and see how often they are updated, as it can vary according to the subject matter and style of the blogger.

You may be thinking "where will I find the time?" If you have chosen a topic that you love, are proud of your blog and the content you are sharing, you will find

Ministry of Type.
http://ministryoftype.co.uk
Aegir Hallmundur is a British designer who blogs about type, typography, lettering, calligraphy, and other related things that inspire him, on this very elegant blog.

Digitising Rare Wood Type

Tuesday 17th May 2011

Signs & Lettering
Tiny Little Details
Type Design

I nearly missed this. One of the Matts at Bearded Design (I'm guessing Matt Griffin) emailed to tell me about their Kickstarter project, which is to create new digital type from wood types - rare wood types. Digitisation of old types is one of those things that thrills some people and gets others in a froth, but I think this is a project that deserves some support. If anything it'll help preserve some wood type designs that might otherwise end up as vile, execrable knick-knacks on Etsy. As they say in films and on TV, you've got 24 hours (as of writing, to get involved early before the project is funded on Kickstarter). Featured below is a 'beta' face they've started digitising, currently called 'Fatboy Husky'. It's available to download through the Kickstarter page.

Fatboy, featured on the Kickstarter page. Kerned (roughly) by me. Ahem.

NEED TO KNOW:
GUEST BLOGGING VS. GHOST BLOGGING

Guest blogging, whether it's someone posting on your blog, or vice versa, is well worth pursuing. It can open the doors to new ideas, new projects, and new collaborations. But the authorship of the post should be made clear.

Something I wouldn't recommend, although it does happen, particularly with business blogs, is getting someone else to blog in your name. This is called "ghost blogging." Although ghost writing is common practice in the print world, the social web is all about openness and authenticity, so pretending to be someone else isn't a great idea. At best, it's fake, and at worst, people may feel cheated if they find out. (And most things get found out on the web!)

the time. But more practically, here are a few ideas of how to keep up your posting frequency:

- *Have a content plan—see Chapter 5: Creating Great Content.*
- *Create several blog posts in one session and schedule them in advance throughout the week or month.*
- *Befriend other bloggers in your field and invite them to "guest post" on your blog occasionally. It takes the pressure off you a little, gives your readers something different, and creates a good relationship with a fellow blogger. (And he or she will probably return the favor.)*
- *Share the load by group blogging.*
- *Manage your readers' expectations. If you're going to be away or too busy to post for a while, explain that in a blog post, then when you get back to blogging you might share what you've been up to and the reason for the blog silence. Blogging is all about transparency and the more honest you are able to be the better. It will help create conversation and a community feeling on your blog.*

EXPERT TIP: **ALOHA LAVINA**

Blog: Imagine That
http://www.pointofutterance.com
Started: 2009
Topic: Photography

"I post at most twice a day and when I am really busy, once a week. At times, when I travel, I can't update my blog for a couple weeks or so. But ideally, I would like to post at least every other day or three times a week. I tend to write a lot of evergreen content—content that makes sense regardless of when you read it—geared towards my photography students, or people who are just starting out with photography as a hobby."

Credentials: Aloha is an editorial and travel photographer based in Asia. As well as authoring her own blog, she contributes to numerous others, including Light Stalking. Her writing and photographs have been featured in *CNNGo* (USA), *UTATA Tribal Photography Magazine* (USA), *Seventeen* (USA), *Estamos!* (Ecuador), *The Korea Times* (South Korea), and several books, including *Danse Avec la Terre*, a photography book for Haiti published in France.

CHAPTER THREE:
STEP-BY-STEP SETUP

Setting up a blog doesn't take long. You can sign up, set up, and publish your first blog post within minutes. I will take you through the setup on three major hosted blog platforms: Blogger, WordPress.com, and Tumblr.

Finding your way around the "back office"

There are at least two sides to a blog: the public face that everyone sees, and the admin screens where you will do most of your work, such as adjusting the settings, writing posts, uploading photos or other media, moderating comments, and adding widgets. When you log in, it's this "back office" that you see. Some blog platforms also allow you to post by emailing in content or via a mobile phone. There is a third side, and that's the "engine." However, the point of blogging software is that you shouldn't have to deal with the technical details; it's all under the hood.

Although all blogging platforms perform more or less the same job, the bad news is that they are all different. You may become a whizz on Tumblr, but WordPress will look like a foreign country. This is why it's a good idea to have a play with at least a couple of platforms before deciding. The type of content you plan to produce will be a big part of your decision.

When you first start there's a lot to take in. The major platforms provide help, but it can be the most basic things—such as how to find the "help" button—that can prove frustrating if you're not used to it.

But now for the good news. One thing common to most platforms, and indeed content management systems generally, is the Edit screen. This is where you type or paste the text content of your blog posts, insert links, upload images, and so on. Some of the icons will

LINK
Any combination of a chain link, sometimes a globe, is the link icon. Highlight the text you want to be hyperlinked, click on this icon, and you will be prompted to insert the link destination.

REMOVE LINK
Highlight the link you wish to remove, and click on this icon.

PHOTO
The photo icon is usually either a little picture or a plain picture frame. Click this to add a photo to a blog post. (Hint: first position your cursor where you want the image to go.)

INSERT VIDEO
Just like the "insert image" icon only with the film strip effect. Sometimes the icon features a video camera rather than a film strip.

be familiar to anyone who uses Microsoft Word, others less obvious. But once you know what to look for, you will find your way around more quickly. Above are some of the key icons to recognize.

This City Never Sleeps.
http://collinkelley.tumblr.com
This is the visual diary of novelist and poet
Collin Kelley's project, a memoir of London.

idsgn. http://idsgn.org
Idsgn describes itself as a blog "about the things
we see and enjoy (or sometimes hate) as designers."
Subjects under discussion include design, branding,
typography, and culture.

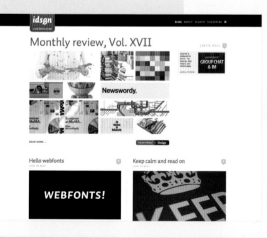

EXPERT TIP: SANDRA MONAT

Blog: HerzensArt
http://herzensart.blogspot.com
Started: 2005
Topic: Craft & Handmade Toys

*"When I started blogging I had just quit my job in the IT business
field, so I did have some technical knowledge. However, when
I stumbled upon the first craft blogs on the internet it felt like a
revelation. I hadn't been in contact with the blogosphere before,
but immediately knew I wanted to be a part of this community
that inspired me so much from the very first minute. That's
when I started my own blog."*

Credentials: Sandra Monat is a full-time designer and artist,
making one-of-a-kind art toys such as Vikings, Knight Templars,
Cowboys, and many more. She uses a variety of materials and
collage techniques and sells her work in an online shop linked
to from her blog.

BLOGGER

Google's Blogger platform has history. In internet terms, you could call it the grandaddy of blogging software since it started in the 20th century (although it's only been a Google property since 2003). Blogger remains the most well-known blogging platform, particularly for hobby and journal bloggers but increasingly also for those looking to make money from their blog. Here are some of the pros and cons.

Pros

- *Long-established and hosted on big, reliable Google servers.*
- *Being part of the Google family means Blogger has some very powerful relations. It integrates seamlessly with Picasa, YouTube, and Google+ for example, and it's easy to display ads on your blog with Google AdSense, which is a significant income stream for some pro bloggers. If you are a Google-head and permanently signed in to Google then you'll undoubtedly find it convenient.*
- *Most people find it simpler to set up and manage than WordPress.*
- *Google continues to improve the service as needs change; for example it now only takes one click to create a version of your blog for smartphones.*
- *Blogs are inserted into the Blogger "blog ring" of sites—the familiar navigation bar at the top of Blogger sites sends you to the next blog in the ring. It's another way of bringing visitors in and adds a nice air of serendipity to Blogger.*

The Crafty Scientist.
http://www.thecraftyscientist.com
Graduate student Mel has only been blogging since January 2011 but has drawn a lot of attention both for her thrifty craft ideas and her eye-catching blog, or rather blogs. This is her main site but she also has a Tumblr blog at http://craftyscientist.tumblr.com

Etsy Vintage Team.
http://etsyvintage.blogspot.com
The Etsy Vintage Team is a group blog for certified vintage sellers on Etsy, featuring tips and sales advice, showcasing members' offerings, and linking to their blogs.

Cons

- *Not everybody loves Google; it has become very large and all-encompassing and Blogger is perhaps less of a community than WordPress or Tumblr.*
- *There is no self-hosted option, so all the content of your blog resides with Google. Although that does not mean Google owns the copyright, it certainly has control over your site.*
- *The default templates aren't very exciting or beautiful, although with some technical input customization is possible.*
- *Blogger does not have categories, but instead you can "label" your posts (a bit like tagging). This can be a problem if you decide to migrate your Blogger blog over to another platform where categories are the norm, because your labels will become categories. As you can imagine, this leaves you with a huge number of random-sounding categories, so some re-filing will be needed.*
- *In some circles there is a certain snobbery about Blogger: people who recall it in the early days may look upon it as being less than professional. But it is still the blog platform of choice for many high-profile and very successful blogs, so you decide!*

TAKE IT FURTHER: A GOOGLE ACCOUNT

A Google account has its benefits. There are many useful Google tools, such as Reader, Docs, Analytics, AdWords, and Webmaster Tools. Not all of these are relevant right now, and some may never be. But you need a Google account to access them. However, the more you use Google, the greater its access to your data. Always read the privacy policy when you sign up for a free service.

EXPERT TIP: TARA MURRAY

Blog: Easy Makes Me Happy
http://easymakesmehappy.blogspot.com
Started: 2009
Topic: Crochet, Craft & Design

"My computer skills were basic, in fact more or less non-existent, so I chose the first free blog host that I came across, which was Blogger. I can't say enough good [things] about it. Starting up is so easy and allows for almost instant blogging with great options for customizing. Once you get started and want to learn more, there are so many resources online to help you."

Credentials: Tara Murray is a wife and a mother of four, who grew up and lives in Alaska. Having an online crochet pattern business (www.mamachee.etsy.com), she started her blog as a way of sharing her craft and other interests, as well as gaining more exposure. Easy is a good example of a blog with real warmth and personality: Tara offers a window into her family and creative life and consequently makes a genuine connection with her thousands of loyal readers.

SETTING UP & POSTING IN BLOGGER

Step 1

When you arrive at Blogger.com you'll have the chance to look around the place before signing up. I recommend taking the short tour before you start, as it gets you ready for what's to come. (There's also a video tutorial if you would prefer to watch that.) At the end of the tour, click on "Get started."

Step 2

This is where you'll be asked to either sign in to your Google account, or sign up for one if you don't yet have one. A Google account is useful for many reasons (see p. 41, Take it Further), and you don't have to have a Googlemail account; you can use any email address to sign up with.

Step 3

The next page will be where you register your blog name and address. It's then just a question of checking whether your name has already been taken. Let's hope not, but if it has, Blogger will suggest some alternatives. Try to avoid going for anything too long or difficult to remember, or with underscores.

Step 4

The final screen in this sequence is "Choose a starter template." It doesn't matter what you choose here as you can always change it later. Just hit "Continue" . . .

Step 5

. . . and you're done! At this point, you could opt to start blogging, but let's click on "Customize how your blog looks . . . "

Step 6

You can now go through the left-hand menu and have a play with your blog's template. At each stage, you will see a preview in the bottom half of the window, but if you want to make the changes you need to hit the "Apply to blog" button.

Step 7

Next, go to "Layout" and you will see a number of choices. If you make changes here you'll probably then want to go back to the "Adjust widths" page.

Step 8

You can adjust the widths of the columns, using the slider bars, or you can specify the widths in pixels. Again, this is all stuff you can change later. Your aim at this stage should be to get familiar with the Blogger "back office" and start to get a feel for what you can do to customize your blog.

Step 9

The final menu item is "Advanced," but don't let that put you off. This is where you can change the font, font colors, and styles for all the different parts of your blog design. You probably won't know immediately what the "Tabs text" or "Post header" is on the page, but once you've written a couple of short test posts you can come back and adjust the design again.

Step 10

Now click "Apply to Blog" and view your blog. How does it look? Probably a little basic, but plenty of room for improvement!

At this point, you could click on "Design" and go back to refining how the blog looks, but a better idea might be to create your first post. It's actually easier to see how your blog is going to look if you have a post or two up there. So click on "New Post."

Step 11

Just type something in the box and have a play with the various editing icons. Some will be familiar but others may not. (See pages 38-39 for an explanation of the typical editing icons you will find across various blogging platforms.)

Step 12

You can also easily create links and upload photos or video. If you have a YouTube or Picasa account you will be able to import your video or photos directly from there. At the foot of the page you will see "Labels." This is where you add any tags, keywords, or phrases that will help people find this post. If you click on "Post Options" you'll see you can allow or disable comments, and you also have the option of scheduling the post in advance rather than posting right away. This is really useful if you are preparing a number of posts in one go. You can click "Preview" at any time to see how it's looking, and when you're happy, click "Publish Post." And that's it!

INSPIRATION: BLOGGER BLOGS

Simply Hue.
http://matissecolor.blogspot.com
Vicki Dvorak is a photographer, artist, and blogger from Seattle, Washington. She began Simply Hue in March 2009 when she was self-employed as a color consultant. Visit Vicki's blog and see her beautiful and unusual photo-montages.

This is Glamorous.
http://citified.blogspot.com
This is Glamorous has a dedicated following of talented and style-savvy readers, including fashionistas, stylists, designers, and the editors of many publications. The blog is a long-time favorite of the editors of *Martha Stewart Living*.

Helt Enkelt.
http://heltenkelthosmig.blogspot.com
Swedish blogger Anna Malin takes gorgeous
photographs of her home and surroundings.
The simple masthead of Helt Enkelt and custom
font for the sidebar headings contribute to the
stylish look of this blog.

Emma Lamb.
http://emmallamb.blogspot.com
Emma calls her blog a "mood board . . . a space for
gathering together all that inspires me in my day
and my crochet work." Her posts are color-themed,
and the blog has attracted attention of both the
mainstream media and other blogs.

helt enkelt...

emma lamb

6 JANUARI 2012
Yummy...

welcome

Anna-Malin heter jag,
fru och mamma till två
pojkar.
Arbetar halvtid som
förskollärare/montesso
ri-
pedagog, och gör
även foto &
stylinguppdrag bl a för
butiker.
Jag älskar allt som är
vackert, att möblera
om, fixa med
olika projekt och att
fotografera förstås.
Vill du boka mig för ett
foto/stylinguppdrag?
Maila mig:
annamalin(a)bredban
d2.com

Varmt välkommen hit.

email me:
annamalin@bredband2.com

follow
me by

thursday, 3 march 2011
fresh spring flowers...

Happy, happy Thursday... !
Other than today's very chilly weather, what is not to be happy about
when there are piles of pretty spring flowers everywhere I look... !?
As soon as I had decided to take part in this craft fair I also decided to
undertake another mammoth task. I'm not sure how this wee idea got
into my head but once it did I just couldn't shift it. This idea was that
I should have a stock of garland flowers waiting in the wings, waiting
for their moment to shine when a custom order would pop into my
inbox... great idea I thought! Of course that was before I did the
maths, if I had done the maths I'm sure I would have thought... 'nah,
bugger it!'

But I didn't, so here I am now living in my wee studio with over four
hundred colourful wee blooms, and then some! Fingers crossed for
some custom orders, eh... !?
This mountain of flowers includes some brand new colours just in time
for the spring. Four gorgeous shades including ~ mustard, silver, soft
pink and soft teal...

Hello my name is Emma Lamb and I
dream in colour... do you?

Follow my blog with Bloglovin

currently loving...
• Sandra Juto's stunning frosty
  windows!
• Golden Spider Silk at the V&A
• Gatherings magazine, The White
  Issue, Winter 2012
• this cute red and white bow jumper at
  Laura Ashley
• my fabulous new Flickr group ~
  making everyday beautiful...

subscribe
  Posts
  Comments

friends & supporters...

links...

EXPERT TIP: **CARA COURAGE**

Blog: Cara Courage

http://www.caracourage.net

Started: 2010

Topic: Arts & Cultural Projects

"My professional website needed to change to one with a content management system, and blogging was an important consideration as I wanted to have a more direct, personal communication with clients and colleagues. So I chose a self-hosted site using software from WordPress.org as the platform for both my blog and my website. It was an issue of cost-saving but also of control and flexibility. It took a while to find a template that I liked, but since then I've found it simple, painless, and quick to work with, and I would recommend it to anyone."

Credentials: Cara Courage is an award-winning arts and culture consultant, entrepreneur, and arts catalyst and enabler. She works with artists and arts organizations, as well as initiating her own collaborative, culturally engaged arts projects.

WORDPRESS

There's one important thing to understand when talking about WordPress, and that is that it has two different personas. I've already mentioned this before, but let's just recap.

WordPress.org began life in 2003 and is the home of blogging software that you have to download, install, and run on your own web space. The software is under continual development and is open-source—in other words, anyone may use and modify it, and they do. It claims that it is the world's largest self-hosting blogging tool.

But the good folks at Automattic (the company behind WordPress) wanted to bring their open-source blogging software to a wider audience, including those with no specialist technical skills, just an enthusiasm to blog. This is how WordPress.com was born.

Inspiredology. http://inspiredology.com
Inspiredology calls itself a "design inspiration lab," curated by Chad Mueller and Andrew Dertinger. The blog is powered by WordPress and hosted at WPWebhost.com.

WordPress.com is a hosted version of the open-source package, with the hosting and managing of the blog software taken care of. In this sense it is more like the other hosted blog platforms, such as Blogger.

In the following pages I will be showing you how to set up a free hosted blog at WordPress.com. But depending on your blogging ambitions and your technical skills, you may wish to consider a self-hosted blog from WordPress.org. A self-hosted blog offers more freedom and flexibility, but it also comes with more responsibility for things like security. Here is a summary of the key benefits and drawbacks of each:

HOSTED BLOG AT WORDPRESS.COM	SELF HOSTED USING BLOGGING SOFTWARE FROM WORDPRESS.ORG
Hosting and managing of software is provided for free.	You need to find and pay for your own hosting.
Very quick and easy to set up.	Technical skills required to set up and manage.
Includes protection against security threats and spam.	You are responsible for your blog's security and spam handling (the software can be vulnerable to hacking).
Although there is a large range of themes (templates) to choose from, they are mostly pretty basic and you can't have a custom theme.	You (or your developer) have complete freedom to create and use custom themes. There are thousands of free themes and plugins available, as well as support forums.
Backups are included, as are software updates.	You have to backup your blog and manually install software updates.
You can't run AdSense-type advertising, except in certain circumstances for highly trafficked blogs.	You can run advertising on your blog.
Sometimes adverts may appear on your blog as WordPress.com reserves the right to do so.	You are in complete control over what displays on your blog, and where.
There are some paid "premium features" available to allow you more flexibility, such as the ability to opt out of displaying adverts or to edit your blog's CSS (the code that controls how your blog displays).	The software isn't just for blogs, it's a complete content management system. So if you are looking for a website as well you could get the whole thing created in WordPress. There are specialist web developers who can do this for you.

SETTING UP & POSTING IN WORDPRESS

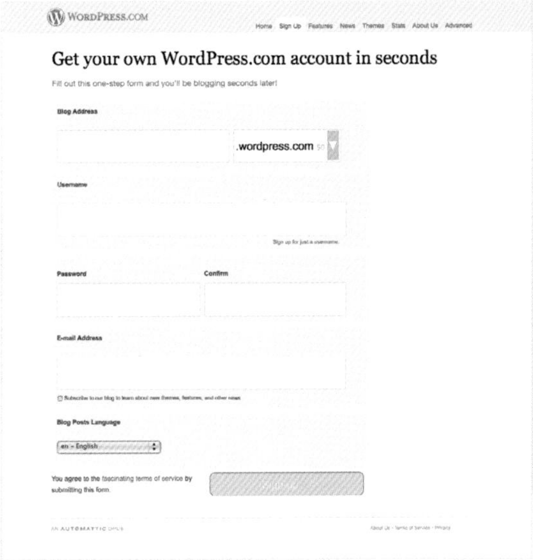

Step 1

Let's look at the steps to setting up a blog at WordPress.com. From the homepage, choose "Sign up" for a new blog and you'll be taken directly to this page.

Enter your chosen blog name, which is what WordPress will give you as a username, but you can create something different for your username if you prefer. There may be a drop-down arrow next to your blog name—if you click this you'll see other possible addresses for your blog. If you stick with yourblogname.wordpress.com then it's free. But for a fee, WordPress will register a domain for you, such as yourblogname.com, if it's available and if you opt for this.

After completing this form you'll have to respond to a confirmation email, and you may be asked to complete your profile at this stage with your name and profile description. You can always go back to this.

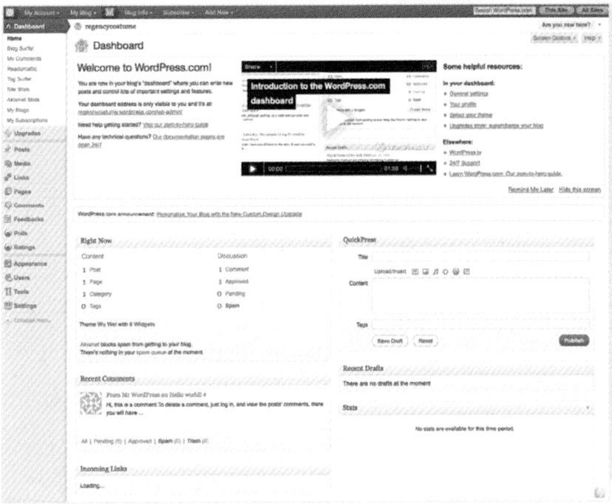

Step 2

The next screen you should see is your blog Dashboard, with a handy short video on how to set it up as you'd like.

I recommend doing one thing right now: make a note of the address of your blog's login page. You'll need to know it to access the admin side of your blog. I've named my example blog regencycostume.wordpress.com, so I log onto it at:

regencycostume.wordpress.com/wp-admin

Take a little while to look around the Dashboard. It won't all make sense right away, but don't be put off. The secret is to learn a little more each time you log on.

Step 3

Your new blog comes with some standard default settings and fillers, for example the tagline "Just another WordPress blog" and a post entitled "Hello World." You could change a few of them right now. Click on "Settings" (at the bottom of the left-hand menu). This will open up the "Settings– General" screen.

The first thing you'll notice is that the blog title is the same as in your blog address. In my case, it's "regency costume." I'd much prefer "Regency Costume," so I can change it here. Next, the tagline is where you can add a short sentence–preferably not too long, as this will appear on the masthead below your blog name. You can also change your time zone and time/date display preferences in this screen.

By default, your blog is public. If you want to make it invisible to search engines, or even completely private, you can do so on the "Settings–Privacy" screen. (Even if you intend to make the blog public, you might want to keep it under wraps until you've finished customizing it.) Be sure to "save changes" at the foot of each page.

Step 4

Your blog will have been assigned a default theme. Click on "Appearance" on the Dashboard menu and you'll be taken to a page where you can browse alternative themes (templates).

There are over a hundred or so to choose from, and that number is being added to all the time. Most are free, but you'll notice there are some "premium" themes, which you have to purchase. We'll look at themes in more detail in the next chapter.

If you decide on a different theme, you can preview how your site will look before commiting. If you like it, click "Activate." You can always change it again!

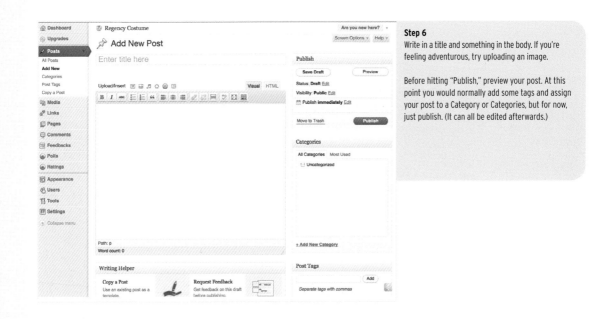

Step 5

There's one more thing to do now, and that's to make your first post. Go to "Posts" in your Dashboard menu, and you'll see something like this.

Where you see "Posts" click on "Add new." This takes you to the screen where you can add or edit your posts.

Step 6

Write in a title and something in the body. If you're feeling adventurous, try uploading an image.

Before hitting "Publish," preview your post. At this point you would normally add some tags and assign your post to a Category or Categories, but for now, just publish. (It can all be edited afterwards.)

My Account ▾   My Blog ▾   W   Blog Info ▾   Subscribe ▾   ★ Like   Add New ▾   Edit

Type here and press enter to search

Regency Costume

HOME   ABOUT

THIS IS MY FIRST POST

Posted by *regencycostume* on July 3, 2011 · *Leave a Comment (Edit)*

Just trying things out around here!

Share this: ✈Tweet   0   📘 *Facebook*

Filed under *Uncategorized*

ARCHIVES

July 2011

META

Site Admin

Log out

Step 7

Now click on "View your post" and see your first WordPress blog post.

At this point you should go back to "Posts" and delete the "Hello, World" post—but before you do, read what it says, as it's a message for you!

NEED TO KNOW: TAGS

Tags are the words and phrases that identify and describe your blog content. Think of the people who would enjoy your blog post. What topics or words might they be searching for? Be specific. If your blog post is a recipe for pumpkin pie, you might tag it with the words pumpkin pie, pie recipe, Thanksgiving, family dessert ideas, that sort of thing. Tagging also helps your blog post to be found by search engines. If this is important to you, make sure your tags appear in the title and/or main body of your blog post, as well as in the "tags" box when you create your post. Tags should be added to all kinds of blog content—video, photos, and audio as well as text entries. In Blogger, tags are called labels.

SEVEN GREAT WORDPRESS PLUGINS FOR SELF-HOSTED BLOGS

If you are setting up a self-hosted blog using WordPress, you have more flexibility and options compared to the hosted version, as I have already mentioned.

But the additional freedom comes with extra responsibilities. For example, you'll need to make sure your blog is secure, free of comment spam, and the software up to date. You will also have to promote your blog—it won't show up as a featured site on WordPress.com or as a recommended blog to follow on Tumblr.

The good news is that there is a large WordPress community of developers continuously working on new plugins. Because WordPress software is open-source, anyone can access it. As a result, there is usually a plugin for the job you need doing: explore the directory at http://wordpress.org/extend/plugins. Here are just a few of the most popular. Some blog hosts offer these (or similar) as one-click installs.

Analytics
Google Analytics. http://www.google.com/analytics
If you are interested in tracking visits to your blog then Google Analytics is free and easy to install on most blogs. You will be able to see where your visitors come from, how long they stay and much, much more. I will go into this in more detail in Chapter 11.

Comment handling
Akismet. http://akismet.com
This plugin filters out potential comment spam and allows you to decide whether it is spam or not. Its settings are adjusted based on your feedback, which means it gets better at filtering over time.

Search engine promotion
All-in-one SEO pack. http://wordpress.org/extend/plugins/all-in-one-seo-pack
If it is important to you that your blog is found by search engines then an SEO (Search Engine Optimization) plugin is a must. It makes it easy to write keyword-rich titles, descriptions, and tags on all your blog posts and pages. (See Chapter 7: Promoting Your Blog for more about this.)

Google XML Site Map Generator for WordPress. http://wordpress.org/extend/plugins/google-sitemap-generator
An XML sitemap is simply an add-on that Google search robots use to find pages and posts on your blog. Having one means your blog has a better chance of being found in searches. Although this is a WordPress plugin, TypePad and Blogger users can opt for an XML sitemap within their dashboard, no extra plugin required.

WeGraphics. http://wegraphics.net
WeGraphics is a creative studio specializing in graphic design resources. An ecommerce plugin allows them to sell directly from their WordPress site.

Security

BackUpWordPress. http://wordpress.org/extend/plugins/backupwordpress

It's essential to back up your blog regularly, like any website. It doesn't matter whether you or your blogging platform provider is hosting your site. Anything could happen and you could lose years of work. For other blogging platforms you will need to check what's available–for example Tumblr has a backup app, but at the time of writing this was only available for Mac OS X.

eCommerce

WP ecommerce. http://wordpress.org/extend/plugins/wp-e-commerce

If you are looking to sell items from your blog, there are many ecommerce plugins out there. WordPress recommends this one as it's "designed with usability, aesthetics, and presentation in mind."

Post photo from Flickr

Flickr Post Photo. http://wordpress.org/extend/plugins/flickr-photo-post/screenshots

With this plugin installed, when you add an image to a post you have the option of uploading one directly from a Flickr album, as well as cropping it in the edit screen.

Akismet. http://akismet.com
Akismet filters out spammy comments so that they don't appear on your blog.

EXPERT TIP: MOLLY WIZENBERG

Blog: Orangette
http://orangette.blogspot.com
Started: 2004
Topic: Food

"When people ask 'who designed your site?' I tell them–I did. I know nothing about coding and next to nothing about computers, but I futzed around (and Googled) until it looked the way I wanted it to. I had heart palpitations the whole time."

Credentials: In the seven years since starting her top-rated blog Orangette, Molly Wizenberg got herself a book deal (a food memoir titled *A Homemade Life*, which made the *New York Times* bestsellers list), a husband, and a restaurant (Delancey in Seattle). Although she describes herself as "crazy-lucky," she also admits to having high standards, and working hard to meet them.

INSPIRATION: WORDPRESS BLOGS

Paper Crave. http://papercrave.com
Kristen Magee admits to "an obsession with stationery, greeting cards, posters and art prints, paper crafts, papercuts, paper sculpture and paper art"... and it's all here at Paper Crave! Kristen's dedication to the blog shows, and with its comprehensive directory of advertisers and suppliers this is clearly an authoritative site.

Grain edit. http://grainedit.com
Grain edit is focused on classic design work from the 1950s-1970s. Founders Dave Cuzner and Elizabeth Surya have built it into a fascinating resource, including interviews, articles, designers' libraries, examples of rare design, and various vintage ephemera. The blog is powered by WordPress using the Tarski Mod Theme.

Strataflora. http://www.strataflora.com
Graphic designer Amy Moore showcases her work and that of others on her blog Strataflora. She created all the graphic elements of the blog and the clean, minimal theme allows the featured work to stand out beautifully.

Sunday Suppers. http://sunday-suppers.com
Sunday Suppers was created by stylist and photographer Karen Mordechai. The blog accompanies the class cooking-dining experiences held in a waterfront loft in Brooklyn, New York. Recipes and restaurant reviews are illustrated with striking photography.

TUMBLR

Tumblr may be the relatively new kid on the block but it is growing in popularity all the time. What's so great about it? For a start, its good looks. This is one cool, minimal blogging tool. Tumblr has a real social feel about it which will be familiar to anyone who is at home with Facebook or Twitter. You can invite friends and easily grab and post content from web pages.

According to the stats, Tumblr appeals to a younger audience, and there's also a slight skew towards male users. So if you or your audience fits that bill you may

Finding Fine Art. http://findingfineart.tumblr.com
This Tumblelog uses the Minimal theme by Artur Kim. It collapses to one column on mobile devices.

PatternBase. http://patternbase.tumblr.com
PatternBase is "a Chicago-based cyber sketchbook dedicated to inspirational textile design and the study of pattern."

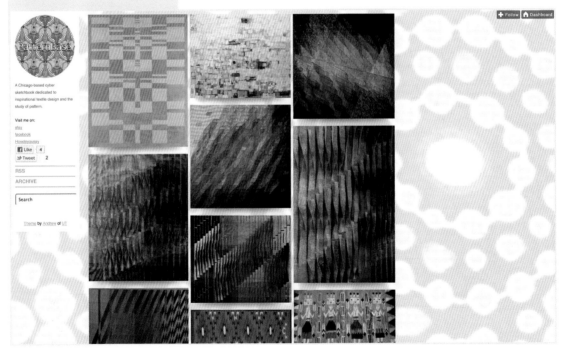

find yourself drawn to it. Many of Tumblr's early issues have been ironed out and there is no doubt it's a vibrant, upcoming platform.

But is it right for you? Here are the pros and cons.

Pros

- *Very simple to set up and manage.*
- *The default themes are nice and simple to style with the colors of your choice. There's a good range of themes in the Tumblr "Theme Garden."*
- *Brilliant for posting photos, video, and audio content. You just select the type of post (photo, text, or whatever) and upload.*
- *Easy to grab extracts from web pages you come across and share on your Tumblelog (as Tumblr blogs are known).*
- *Most Tumblr themes are designed to automatically display properly when viewed on a smartphone.*
- *Comes with a Dashboard so you can easily see recent posts by those you follow, rather like Facebook's newsfeed.*
- *Can be used as a lightweight, secondary, or micro-blog, alongside something heftier on WordPress, for example.*
- *Very social—it's a community focused on sharing (re-blogging) and liking people's posts, and links to your Twitter and Facebook are standard.*

Cons

- *You can't self-host your blog—it sits on the Tumblr server, so if it goes down you go down with it.*
- *With such simplicity and ease of use it's inevitable that there are sacrifices. Some widgets and plugins that come included on other blog platforms have to be manually added in Tumblr.*
- *Tumblr doesn't have comments—readers have to be satisfied with either "liking" a post or re-blogging it, which may not be obvious to non-Tumblr users. However, you can install a comments plugin called Disqus that does the job.*

EXPERT TIP: JOHN MARTZ

Blogs: John Martz & Drawn

http://notebook.johnmartz.com & http://blog.drawn.ca

Started: 2003

Topic: Design & Illustration

"Switching to Tumblr was a matter of efficiency. As a Tumblelog, my content is more of a freeform stream of images, videos, links, and text snippets. That means I no longer think of each post as an article that needs a title and a certain amount of content. It allows me to share the things I make and am interested in without the pressure of format. Tumblr makes blogging feel less like editing a magazine and more like collecting neat stuff in a shoebox."

Credentials: John Martz is an illustrator, designer, and cartoonist living in Toronto. He has been blogging since 2003, initially as Robot Johnny. As well as his own blog, he blogs with six other creatives at Drawn, which describes itself as a "daily source of inspiration for illustration, animation, cartooning, and comic art."

SETTING UP & POSTING IN TUMBLR

Step 1
Here's where you get started with Tumblr.com. On the homepage, fill in your email address, choose a password, and type in your chosen blog name. It will look like:

blogname.tumblr.com

If your blog name has been taken you'll be asked to choose again. If it is free, the next screen might be a Captcha (to check that you are human), and then you'll be prompted to create your first post.

Step 2
First post? Already?? Yes, Tumblr doesn't want you to spend too long thinking about this–just do it! You'll notice that there is a different button for each type of post–text, photo, quote, link, chat, audio, and video. You might want to try clicking on each option in turn (you can use your browser's "back" button each time to go from one to the other) and see what comes up. You'll then get a feel for what you can put on your blog and any limitations Tumblr imposes, for example, on the amount of video and audio you are allowed to post each day. Get the picture? Now it's time to post something. (Note: you will need to check your email at this point and verify your address.)

Posting to your Tumblr blog

1. To make your first post, try clicking on "Text." On the screen will come a series of boxes–type in something in the "Title" box, then under "Post" write whatever you want.

2. Click on "Preview" to see how it will look. Don't worry if the page looks a bit empty and boring at this point, you can customize it later.

3. Before publishing, decide whether you are happy for people to reply with a photo, and if you are then check the "allow photo reply" box.

4. There's one other thing you should get into the habit of doing, and that's adding tags to your post. Type them into the "tags" box. These are keywords to help people find your post and others like it. (See p. 53, Need to Know, for more about tags.)

5. When you're happy with your post, hit "Create post." You can also choose to schedule it for the future, save it for now, or publish it privately–to do this, choose from the drop-down menu where it says "publish now."

Step 3

Congratulations! Your first post is up–this next screen will invite you to "Customize your blog."

First off your blog needs a title and you're asked to upload a photo. As with any web avatar (the picture that appears next to your posts and comments, Twitter and Facebook updates, and so on) you can use a photo of yourself or something that represents you. You can do this later if you don't have one ready to upload.

Click on "Show all appearance options;" you are taken to a page that looks like this (below):

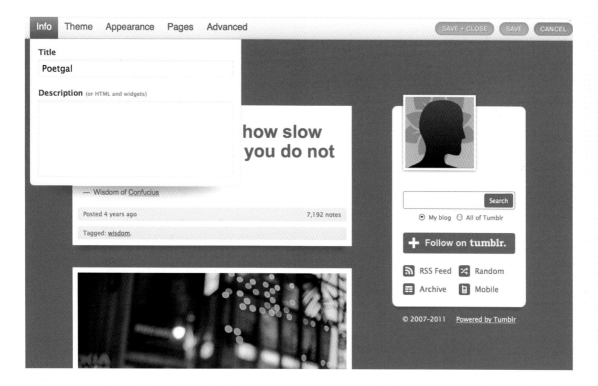

HERE'S WHAT YOU CAN DO UNDER THE MENU OPTIONS:

Info
Enter (or change) the title of your blog and write a short (one sentence) description of what it's about.

Theme
Here's where you change the look of your blog. The first themes on show are "premium," in other words, not free. Scroll down to find the free themes—there are plenty of good ones. When you find one you like, go ahead and click, you will then see how the page looks with this theme. Try a few out before deciding.

Appearance
What you see will depend on the theme you have chosen. You can style your theme by changing certain aspects of it. Usually this includes things like font color and background color, and if the theme has plugins already installed, such as Google Analytics, Disqus (for comments), or a Twitter feed, this is where you fill in your username or account details.

Pages
Here you can add a page—for example, "About," or "Portfolio," or whatever content you'd like on a static page (as opposed to your blog posts).

Advanced
If you (or someone you know) understands code then this is where you can add some "custom CSS"—this will override aspects of the theme and customize your blog even further, but you need a bit of technical know-how. If in doubt, leave blank. The other options here are the number of posts you want to display per page, whether or not you want your blog to be optimized for display on a mobile phone, and so on. If you're not sure, go with the pre-selected options.

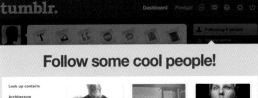

Step 4
When you've finished customizing your blog, click SAVE. You can come back to this page any time once you're logged in, by going to "Preferences" in your Dashboard (cog icon) and "Customize."

Once you "Save and Exit" from this screen, you'll be prompted to "Follow some cool people"—which is a great way to start connecting with other Tumblelogs. Look for your category and browse.

When you hover your mouse over a blog, a little "follow +" button will appear—just click on this to follow them. (Be aware that if you click on the blog to have a look at it first, you will be taken away from your current screen as the blog will open in the same window.)

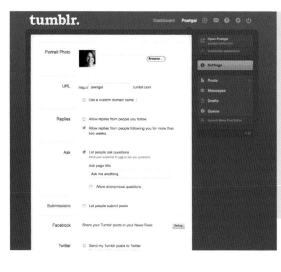

Step 5

From your Dashboard, click on your blog name on the top menu and select "Settings."

Take a moment to work through the options here, such as time zone, privacy, whether you want your Tumblr posts to go to your Twitter feed, that sort of thing. If you're not sure about anything, leave the default settings and you can always find out about this later.

That's it—start blogging, re-blogging, and following interesting people!

Dashboard

Your Dashboard is the screen you see each time you log in, and it will display a rolling feed of posts from the Tumblelogs you follow. On the top right is a menu.

The icon on the far right is the "logout" button. The "plus sign" is if you want to create a new Tumblelog. The question mark is where you go for help: Tumblr is a large, supportive community and you should get any answers you need here. If you receive a message there will be a red number against the "mail" icon, and the "cog" takes you to Preferences.

Reblogging

When readers like what you've posted on Tumblr, they can "like" it or "reblog" it. Reblogging means it then appears intact on that person's Tumblelog, fully credited and with all its notes, which you can see in this example. In this way, Tumblelogs are quickly brought to the attention of new audiences.

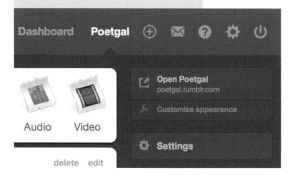

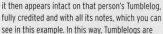

INSPIRATION: **TUMBLELOGS**

Urban Modernista.
http://www.urbanmodernista.com
Katrine Wallace's vintage-themed Tumblelog, Urban
Modernista, features modern design, vintage scooters,
60s pop culture, and mod fashion.

Mareen Fischinger.
http://blog.mareenfischinger.com
German Photographer Mareen Fischinger blogs about
her work, "behind the scenes," and personal life. The blog
uses the minimalist Scaffold theme by Mike Harding,
which has a static left-hand sidebar while the main
body of the page scrolls.

Brushes with Strangers.
http://brushes-with-strangers.tumblr.com

When Mike Reed started sketching fellow commuters on his iPad and posting them on Facebook, enough people were interested for him to start this blog. The theme is by Handsome Code.

Mark Karwowski.
ihttp://markkarwowski.tumblr.com

Graphic design student Mark Karwowski uses his Tumblelog as a "creative diary," revealing both what interests him in the area of design but also his own creations. He uses the Effector theme by Carlo Franco.

CHAPTER FOUR:
CREATING AN EYE-CATCHING BLOG

What's the secret of great blog design? At its heart are many of the principles of good graphic design. There are some key differences between screen and print, for example in the way that colors, graphics, and text are displayed. We also process what we're seeing and interact with it differently on screen.

Attention to design will give your blog a strong, consistent visual feel in which the right things are emphasized and the viewer quickly makes sense of what's there. It sounds unfair, but on our first visit to a blog we all make instant judgements about whether we like it, what we think of its subject matter and its owner—all in a split second!

When making design choices, you will naturally be guided by your blog's subject matter and content. If you are seeking commercial success or if your blog is part of your business, consider also your audience and its expectations. But if you are blogging for your own satisfaction or in connection with a hobby, there's no need to think like a marketer—do whatever pleases you and your enthusiasm will shine through!

There are many thousands of professionally created templates, or themes, available for your blog. Some you can customize a little, others are customizable to the nth degree, if you have the know-how.

You could even employ the services of a developer who can make your theme unique or create a new one for you from scratch. This is because blog platforms such as WordPress have made their software open source (see Need to Know, opposite). Take a look at the portfolio of any designer you are considering to see

Hendra Lauw. http://www.hendralauw.com
The blog of Singapore-based photographer Hendra Lauw creates a stunning effect straight off with the use of big, bold photos from her portfolio.

what they have done for others and whether you like their style.

But hold on a moment, if you're reading this book then you're a creative person, right? So you probably want a big say in how your blog turns out. Are you comfortable with sketching out how you want something to look, or using image-manipulation tools onscreen such as Adobe Photoshop? If you're a designer or typographer, then probably yes—but for those of us more skilled in the written word, or sculpture, or cookery . . . not necessarily.

There are many forms of creativity. When it comes to what works visually on the web, it can be a whole new ball game. I've encountered all kinds of creatives over the years and believe me, even the greatest graphic designer can come to grief on web design!

So what's so different about designing for the web? I'm not talking about the technical aspects of web design to do with coding, but purely the visible aspects of the page: the layout and content.

Whether you're customizing a standard theme yourself using the drag-and-drop dashboard of your blog platform, or whether you're designing how your blog needs to look from scratch for a developer to code up, it's useful to have a little knowledge about color, typography, layout, design conventions, web peculiarities, and generally what works. You'll feel more confident about the end result and it will be more professional and eye-catching than the majority of blogs out there!

In this chapter you will learn more about why some designs work better than others and some key web design principles. I will also give you some tips on how to customize the design of your chosen theme or template.

Recipe Girl. www.recipegirl.com
Lori Lange's Recipe Girl blog focuses on great food photography and catches your attention with a rotation of featured articles center-top below the header banner.

NEED TO KNOW: OPEN SOURCE

The term "open source" in relation to software refers to something that has been developed not by one person or company but by many. WordPress, for example, allows developers access to its source code so that it may be liberally used, altered, and re-written by anyone with the skills to do so. The philosophy behind open-source software is that by allowing people to freely access and alter the code, it is enriched and developed collaboratively, and everyone benefits from the improved product.

MAKING BEST USE OF COLOR

One of the beauties of designing for the web, as opposed to print, is that you can try things out before committing to them. This is great news if, like me, you're not always 100% confident about which colors will work together. On the other hand, you may already have a good idea of the colors you like and would like to use on your blog. Either way, it's worth experimenting a little. You will be amazed at the difference a subtle color adjustment can make.

Luckily, gone are the days when web designers had to worry about using "web safe" colors. The problem was that computer screens were only capable of displaying a limited range of colors, so if you wanted your colors to look like you intended you needed to choose from a range of 216. This may sound like a lot, but trust me, it's not!

You don't need the knowledge of a fine artist to use a web color picker. But it's helpful to bear in mind a few rules of thumb.

For example, generally speaking warm colors, such as red or orange, will appear to jump out at you, whereas blues, greens, and other colors on the "cool"

Adobe Kuler. http://kuler.adobe.com
In Kuler you can experiment and save your schemes. Others can comment on them, which is a great way of getting feedback.

Color Palette Generator
http://www.degraeve.com/color-palette
Color Palette Generator is a simple tool for identifying the color palette behind a photo.

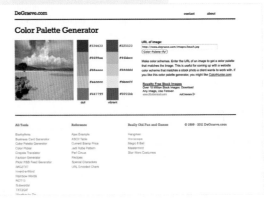

Adobe Kuler is a popular tool. At Kuler you can create your own color themes, see those made by others, and rate them. Even if you have no idea about which colors go together, you can play around and see which combinations are pleasing, saving the ones you like.

Color Palette Generator is a great tool for creating a color palette from a photograph. Just type in the web address of the photo and it comes up with a complementary palette. Simple idea; very useful tool!

spectrum tend to recede. That means you need very little of a warm color to achieve a contrast.

Always consider the effects of looking at a back-lit screen—certain colors and color combinations can be difficult to read. It can also be hard work to read light-colored text on a dark background.

When you visit other websites, start noticing the color combinations used for background, headings, body copy, borders, and other elements on the page. Do they work well? If not, what would you do differently?

Of course, rules can always be broken and sometimes to great effect!

There are a number of fantastic web tools to help you make color choices and experiment with different combinations. You don't have to understand the science behind it, and it's a great way of developing your eye for color. Just messing around with colors can be an inspiration in itself. Many color tools are free to use, and here are three of my favorites: Adode Kuler, Color Palette Generator, and Color Scheme Designer.

Color Scheme Designer
http://colorschemedesigner.com
With just two or three clicks you can generate a complementary color palette.

The same color palette previewed as a web page. You can change around the colors within this view.

Color Scheme Designer is a very neat tool developed by Czech web designer Petr Stanicek. It's very easy to see with a click which colors complement one another. You can also preview how your color scheme would look on a web page, and export your color schemes for you or your web designer to use in a blog template. You can even see how your color scheme looks to someone on the spectrum of color blindness.

TYPOGRAPHY: WHAT DO THE WORDS LOOK LIKE?

Sad to say, typography (not just the typeface, but also the balance of letterforms on the page) is the "poor relation" of web design. What I mean is that it just doesn't get the attention it deserves and is often the last thing to be considered, if at all.

In the early days of the web, HTML (the original markup code in which websites were written) was not created with visual design in mind, let alone the subtleties of typography as it existed in the print world.

Text on web pages was displayed according to default settings, with body copy in a serif font such as Times New Roman.

It was possible for web designers to specify alternative typefaces and font styles, but not until the development of something called Cascading Style Sheets (CSS) did it become easy to manipulate letter spacing, line heights, and absolute positioning of elements on the page.

Naomie Ross / Design x Motion / New York. http://www.naomie.me.
It's worth looking at how typefaces are used in advertising or in signage we take for granted. Designer Naomie Ross created this inspirational book from photos of signs she found around Coney Island.

NEED TO KNOW: SERIF vs. SANS SERIF
Serifs are the little details on the ends of letters. Sans serif fonts (from the French "without") are smoother and cleaner.

MOTION

2011 Reel
Letterpress
City of Melbourne Logo ID
Good Eats Show Open
There Will Be Blood Title Sequence
Self Portrait

PRINT

SVA Motion Graphics Show Posters
Gogol Book Set
Pardon my French Clarendon
Blown a Wish Vinyl Record
Lovechild Typeface
Robot-Themed Wedding
Vivaldi: The Four Seasons
Anatomy of Type
Angels in America
La Vie Bohème
No One Belongs Here More Than You
NY Times Layout
Coney Island Typography
Hockey News
J.D. Salinger Book Set

INFO

Resume
Email: hello[at]naomie.me
LinkedIn

Copyright 2011

CONEY ISLAND TYPOGRAPHY BOOK

I walked around Coney Island and photographed signs that I thought were interesting, I then brought them into photoshop, manipulated the images to my liking and created a color scheme for the whole book.

 Prev | Next   6/13

TAKE IT FURTHER: TYPEFACE VS. FONT

Purists may have noticed that I am using the terms typeface and font almost interchangeably. This is because the lines between the two are rather blurred when talking about the web. Strictly speaking, the typeface is the family to which the fonts belong. Helvetica is a typeface, but Helvetica Italic 11pt is a font. Nonetheless, in web markup language we speak of font families, font weights, font styles and so forth.

Fonts

How text is rendered on screen still depends on the complex interplay between the computer's operating system and web browser, and the web server where the page is hosted. This is why so many web pages fall back on standard default typefaces, typically Arial, Verdana, or Helvetica—all sans serif fonts which are generally considered to be clearer to read on screen. This is different from how typefaces are used in print magazines, and newspapers, where headlines are typically in sans serif and the body copy in serif.

Letters on a screen will also never be as crisp and precise as their printed equivalents, because they are lower resolution (far fewer dots per inch). But that doesn't mean you cannot create a beautiful, stunning effect with typography.

New fonts are being designed all the time, as well as new versions of classic typefaces. A web search will throw up thousands of websites with fonts for download, many of them free. Beware though: an obscure font won't necessarily display properly on another computer.

Lovely Stationery. http://lovelystationery.com
The Lovely Stationery blog, with a simple logo and use of white space, keeps things clean by using the sans serif font Arial in a warm gray color for both headings and body copy.

Nerdist. http://www.nerdist.com
The Nerdist makes good use of the Typekit font Atrament-Web, a narrow typeface well suited to situations where the text needs to make an impact in a small amount of space.

We Make Words.
http://wemakewords.blogspot.com
Illustrators Amy Borell and Luci Everett run a blog
project based on graphic interpretations of words.
The handwritten-style sidebar is a very nice effect.

Uppercase. http://uppercase.squarespace.com
Be sure to explore the Typography category
at Calgary-based blog Uppercase—a community
for "the creative and the curious" and a
companion site to *Uppercase* magazine.

TAKE IT FURTHER: HOSTED FONTS

Historically, one of the problems with specifying the fonts
for websites was that it depended on what fonts the user's
computer had installed. If a web designer specifies "Bernard
MT Condensed" and that font isn't installed on your machine,
when you look at the site you will see a default font in its
place, such as Arial or Times New Roman. The issue can be
avoided by using hosted fonts, such as those provided by
Typekit (http://typekit.com). By subscribing to Typekit you
can choose from a library of fonts, safe in the knowledge
that your chosen font will render consistently in different
browsers and on any individual computer.

Spacing

In the language of typography, the spacing of letters is
called tracking or kerning and the spacing of lines is
leading. You will find these terms if you use any kind of
image-manipulation software such as Adobe Photoshop,
but you may also see it called plain old letter-spacing
and line-height.

Even small tweaks to the letter and line spacing
can have a big effect on the impact of your blog both in
practical terms (such as readability) and stylistic effect.

The use of space is a powerful element of design,
and on screen is no exception. Don't feel you have to fill
up every available space.

TEMPLATES & THEMES

You will often see "template" and "theme" used interchangeably. This is how I will use the terms now, because in many cases they mean pretty much the same thing, although they're not strictly speaking the same (a template implies a pre-designed visual layout whereas a theme includes more elements than this).

Think of your template as being the shell of a house. The walls have been built, the size of the rooms decided, the windows, doors, and roof all put in position. It will have a shape and a structure which cannot be changed, but everything else is yours to make your own. It may have some basic decoration to it already, but you are still free to re-paint walls, hang drapes or blinds, decide where the furniture will go, and what you will grow in the yard.

Different themes or templates will allow different degrees of customization. This is perhaps one of the hardest aspects of choosing a theme—knowing or finding out what what can and can't be changed. My advice is to start with a relatively simple theme and if you find yourself growing out of it you can change it. You may even want to experiment with a "test" blog for a while, before committing to a theme. The more flexible and customizable the theme, the more likely you are going to need some technical know-how or help from a web developer to make it how you want it.

You can choose a theme by category or style, by color palette, or by popularity. Start with the themes or templates developed by your chosen blogging software platform, and if you're not inspired then search for "WordPress Themes" or whatever platform you are using. Thousands of results will come up. Be careful with free themes from unknown providers—a better bet from the point of view of stability, security, and support is to pay a few dollars for a "Premium" theme.

Elements of a theme that are usually very easy to change are colors (of backgrounds, fonts, borders, and

Themes. http://www.wordpressthemes.com
If you want something a little different there are hundreds of Premium Themes (not free) to choose from, either from designers or via theme catalog and review sites, such as this.

so forth), logos, and photos. Sometimes you can choose between different layout options (number of columns, for example), change font families, styles and sizes, graphical elements, and mastheads. You can usually suppress elements you don't want. Some themes work with certain plugins and others don't.

Even if it's not obvious how to change something in a template, it can still be possible. Many of the most popular WordPress themes, for example, have communities of users who contribute to a growing body of help and support. With a smaller theme you can usually contact the developer and ask a question.

Let's look at what you can do to your theme to make it more your own, without having any special technical knowledge.

TIPS FOR CUSTOMIZING A THEME

There are three levels to customizing a theme or template. The first involves finding your way around the template elements of your blog dashboard and using the editing tools available.

The second level is for those who are happy to learn a few new skills and get their hands a little dirty. Level three is getting under the hood and fiddling about with the code: but beware! You need to know what you're doing.

As an example, I am using the proto-blog Blogging for Creatives on Blogger.com that I set up in Chapter 3. Although you may not be using Blogger, much of the terminology and editing process is similar across different platforms.

Step 1
To begin editing a template, look for the words "Template," "Design," or "Layout" on your dashboard. In Blogger, choose "Template" from the left-hand menu, then "Customize," which takes you to the Template Designer screen. Your blog homepage appears in the bottom section of the screen, with the editing tools and menus on top. At the moment, my blog has the "Simple" template default blue background and header title in Arial.

Step 2
I'm not keen on that, so I go through the left-hand menu playing with the colors for the background and header section. Then under "Advanced" I experiment with colors and font styles used in the title and subheading. Eventually I decide on this.

Step 3

It looks a little narrow to me. By selecting "Adjust widths" from the left-hand menu I can change the widths of the columns (and the overall width) using the sliders.

The template is now 940 pixels wide, which may be too wide for some screens—you may want to keep yours to 800 pixels, although you will find more and more websites run on wider formats as monitors get bigger and screen resolution higher.

I decide to have a banner across the top, rather than the text. I make it the same as the overall width, 940 px, and 200 px in height. (Beware of making it too deep, as it will push your content down the page.)

Step 4

Once I have created my banner, I go to the Template Editor and choose "Layout." I select "Edit" where the header is, and the "Configure Header" window appears. I then browse to my banner on my computer, select "Instead of Title and Description" and hit "Save." Trouble is, now my background color looks wrong! So I go back into the Template Editor and change to a yellow-ish green.

I now have a basic template with a little customization and it took less than an hour, including the banner (see Chapter 5 for more about photo editing).

- *Decide when enough is enough—tweaking a design can take over and you will never be "finished," so stick with a template, see whether people like it, and let it "bed down." You can always make tweaks but if the site is always changing it will disorientate people.*
- *Explore widgets and plugins—if there's something you want to have on your blog, like a poll or a Twitter feed, look for something ready-made.*
- *Know your limitations—too much tinkering can result in things breaking, so ask for help from a developer before it comes to that.*
- *Back up your blog regularly and certainly before making any major changes to the template.*

If you want to learn about CSS (Cascading Style Sheets), which is the language in which colors, fonts, layout, and spacing are specified, you can take customization a lot further. But for now, here are a few basic principles to remember when customizing your blog's template:

CHAPTER FIVE:
CREATING GREAT CONTENT

This is it—the heart of your blog! You're open for business, you've got a unique identity for your blog, so now there's no excuse not to start posting all that fabulous content you've been burning to share.

Think back on what I mentioned in Chapter 1—the majority of all blogs are abandoned within three months. The most common excuse offered by lapsed bloggers is lack of time. But really, how much time does it take to upload a photo, or write a hundred words on something you really love and think about every day?

I have certainly started blogs that have fallen by the wayside, but it's not normally for lack of time; rather for lack of planning ahead. It's thinking about what to post that often takes up the time—not the actual posting.

No matter how passionate you are about your subject, there will always be days when you look at the blank box on the screen and your heart sinks. What to post? Perhaps you're at a crucial stage with a project and blogging isn't really at the top of your mind. Or all the ideas you think of you feel you've done before. This is when a content plan will save you. Just reminding yourself of all those great blog ideas you had a couple of weeks ago, or reviewing your most popular posts can spark your imagination.

Or perhaps you have the opposite problem—rather than bloggers' block you are presented with another common issue: "How do I choose what to blog about when I have so much to say?" Knowing how to pace yourself, and how to present your content in ways that

Rachel Lucie. http://blog.rachellucie.co.uk
The blog of jewelry designer Rachel Lucie features not only her work, but things that inspire her, from views of the countryside from her window to fashion photography.

will delight your readers and keep them coming back, without overloading them; these are all things you will get better at, by building them into your content strategy. The more you blog, the more you will learn about what people enjoy about your blog. Yes, there are types of blog posts that have been shown time and time again to be popular. But the trick is to find the balance between following formulas and creating something unique and lasting of your own.

In this chapter I will share with you the secrets of the top bloggers—where they come up with the ideas and the material, how they plan out their content, and what makes a great blog post. We will also look at posting video and audio content to your blog.

LEARN TO RETOUCH

12 BLOG POSTS THAT WORK

There are certain kinds of blog posts that have been proven to work. Here are some of them. You can refer back to these pages when you're feeling stuck for ideas.

1. List

The page you are reading, if it were on a blog, is an example of a "list" post. There's something about a list that always seems to attract readers. For example, it could be a "top ten," or "seven things you never knew about X," or perhaps "three reasons to do Y." People love to see themselves mentioned favorably on a blog, especially if it's a "top ten," so this kind of post, used occasionally, will win you some instant friends!

2. Story

Any writer will tell you that stories sell. Stories take us on a journey—think about when you were a child listening to a story, desperately needing to know what happens next. If a story is told well, it takes us back to that state of concentration. A story post might be, "How I created X," or "What I learned when I tried Y." If you can present a problem and show how it was tackled, great. Case studies are always popular. Keep it simple: situation, dilemma/issues, action, outcomes.

3. "How to" / practical advice

Share your expertise! Everybody loves to learn from others, especially when it comes in the form of practical tips. This kind of post lends itself well to video—it's great to watch something demonstrated. There's more about video blogging later in this chapter. Remember, there are many, many people with no idea how to do what you do, and there is plenty you can teach them without giving away all your secrets!

PadStyle. http://padstyle.com
PadStyle is a decor blog with posts on stylish home furnishings. This post, "25 top interior design and furniture blogs," is a great example of a list post that also serves as a review post.

4. Photo

On a creative blog you can't beat a photo, or photos. Make them big, beautiful, and interesting, and sometimes a one-word caption is all that's needed.

5. Point of view / "my take"

Got a point of view? Your blog is your voice, and if you use it authentically to comment on what you see going on in your industry or what you're enjoying at the moment, others will join in the discussion. People will get to know you through these types of posts, so although you may not feel able to bare your soul, don't be shy about saying what you think. You don't have to be controversial, just be yourself through your blog. Which brings me to the next point . . .

6. Controversy

If you thrive on debate, by all means play devil's advocate and turn up the temperature! Just make sure you can stand the heat. You need to be able to deal with rude comments and not take them personally. In the old internet days there were things called "flame wars." I've seen some shocking online spats on anything from using fois gras in a recipe, to whether or not Helvetica is the "best" typeface.

7. Review / preview

Reviewing used to be something that only professionals would do: think Siskel and Ebert. Now, we all read reviews posted by ordinary people on sites like TripAdvisor.com and Amazon.com and think nothing of it. Everyone's a reviewer now! Whether you're reviewing or previewing a restaurant's food, a designer's work, an exhibition, a gadget launch . . . people want your take on it, as it saves them having to do the research. If they are regular readers of your blog, they are also likely to value your opinion over that of a stranger. Note: if you accept compensation for a review then you need to be upfront about that or it may damage your credibility. More about this later in the book.

Mochimochi Land.
http://www.mochimochiland.com
Anna Hrachovec uses photo sequences to show knitting techniques to her blog audience.

How to: Knitting with Double-Pointed Needles

Knitting with double-pointed needles, or DPNs, is an excellent way to knit 3-dimensional toys with minimal seaming. The needles, which are usually used 4 at a time, take a little getting used to, but it's really less complicated that it looks! This tutorial will show you the DPN basics when knitting toys.

Using DPNs with a large number of stitches
If you haven't used DPNs before, start out by practicing with a large number of stitches.

1. Cast all of the stitches onto one needle. Then, distribute the stitches onto 3 needles by slipping some of them purlwise onto 2 more needles. Hold the needles so that the yarn is attached to the needle on the right and lies behind that needle, and all of the stitches are aligned on the inside of the needles.

2. If you will use a stitch marker to keep track of the beginning of your rounds (I recommend it), then place the marker on the right needle, next to the stitch with the yarn attached. For this first stitch only, knit directly from the left needle to the right, joining the stitches together into a round as you do so.

3. Next, pick up a fourth needle, and use it to knit the stitches on the left needle. Just let all the

Follow Us On Twitter

Anna Hrachovec
2483 followers

- UNIQLO's Army of Sheep: I was greeted by this display last month when I stopped by UNIQLO, one of my favorite cl... http://t.co/rvofmUv8 about 15 hours ago
- @smithnikki Thanks for the RT!! about 15 hours ago
- Just got the coolest squishiest thing! It will be one of the Mochimochi Photo Contest prizes!! about 16 hours ago
- RT @susanbanderson: Wee Ones – Seamless Knit Toys! My new @beCraftsy online course is available for 50% off for a short time "... about 22 hours ago
- @kwilbi WOW about 1 day ago
- @mightyjune Thanks for sharing! about 1 day ago

8. Contest / giveaway

Readers love giveaways and contests. If you are just building your readership you may not get many participants, but don't be put off. Some bloggers run regular contests and giveaways to help grow their readership and stimulate activity on the blog. Don't be in a hurry to give away something you would otherwise sell. Give away other people's stuff as prizes. As your blog audience grows, so will your attractiveness to potential advertisers and fellow bloggers alike, so getting hold of prizes shouldn't be a problem. (More about this in Chapter 9.) But be careful: make sure your contest is compliant with advertising regulations.

9. Interview / profile

Do you get to go to conferences or industry meetups, first nights or previews? Why not approach someone interesting and ask to interview them? It may be a fellow artist, practitioner, enthusiast, blogger, or even just someone you work with or admire. Have a few open questions to ask them, and post the interview on your blog. You could interview them on video, or on the phone (from which you could make an audiocast), or even by Twitter or email.

10. Prediction

If you've always got an eye on what's new and like to stay ahead of things, demonstrate that with the occasional prediction post. January is the obvious month for predictions, but don't be limited by that. Got a hot tip about what's going to be big in six months? Share it. And be sure to revisit your post in six months' time to see if you were right!

PaperCrave. http://papercrave.com
PaperCrave demonstrates its authority and helps promote blogger and designer Tara Hogan of Ink + Wit (http://inkandwit.blogspot.com) by giving readers a preview of what she will be offering at an upcoming Stationery Show.

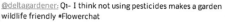

{LIFE on the BALCONY}

Flower Chat: What Flowers Attract Birds, Bees, and Butterflies?

by FERN *on* AUGUST 18, 2011
in BIRDS BEES & BUTTERFLIES, FLOWER CHAT

The following is the transcript of our Flower Chat held on August 18, 2011. The chat was moderated by yours truly (@lifeontheblcny). Our guest was Dave Bushnell (@BushnellGardens), the owner of Bushnell Gardens Nursery in Granite Bay, CA. We discussed attracting wildlife like birds, bees, and butterflies to the garden.

Thanks to everyone who participated in the discussion!

- Q1 Are there some general rules for making a flower garden wildlife-friendly?
- Q2 Ladybugs are always fun to see in the garden, and they eat pests! Are there flowers that attract ladybugs?
- Q3 What are some drought tolerant plants that will also attract birds, bees, or butterflies?
- Q4 Many people know asclepias attracts butterflies, but what are some other butterfly-friendly plants?
- Q5 Are there any shade flowers that attract hummingbirds?
- Q6 Do we need to think about supporting bees in the fall and winter? If yes, how can we do that?

 @Flower_Chat: Q1 - Are there some good general rules for making a flower garden wildlife-friendly? #flowerchat

 @vagablonde515: @jchapstk hi #Flowerchat

 @deltagardener: Q1- I think not using pesticides makes a garden wildlife friendly #Flowerchat

@jchapstk: RT @deltagardener: Q1- I think not using pesticides makes a garden wildlife friendly #Flowerchat

@jchapstk: @vagablonde515 Hi. #Flowerchat

 @BushnellGardens: A1: We think so. Each region differs however integrating flowerful plants; nativies and non-natives is a good start. #flowerchat

11. Round-up

A round-up can be a collation of articles you've recently read, of people you met at an event, or talks you heard at a conference, that sort of thing. It's a cross between a review and a list. This can be a bit of a fallback if you're stuck for original content one day, although it can also be informative in itself, especially if you have a theme and put your own take onto material you feature (rather than just a list of links).

12. Something different

Mix things up every now and then. If you tend to post mainly written articles, why not try the odd video post for a change? If many of your blog posts are in-depth pieces, throw in the occasional short post, or even just a photo with an invitation to comment. Professional bloggers will tell you to always stay on topic, but if you are a hobby blogger, feel free to sometimes post about something else, if that's what's on your mind.

ANATOMY OF A COMPELLING BLOG POST

So just what separates a mediocre blog post from one that is awesome?

You have an advantage: if you're reading this book you are most probably a creative person with plenty of ideas for making your blog unique. Nonetheless, there are some specific features to a blog post that will help ensure that it is read, enjoyed, and shared. Let's take a look at these essential elements.

Headline

On a business blog, the headline you choose is all-important, because people will decide very quickly on the basis of your headline whether or not to click through and read. On the other hand, descriptive headlines often work perfectly well for creative blogs, especially if the blog content is visuals-led. You don't have to be ultra cute with your headlines, but you do want your blog to stand out from the crowd. Ask yourself: would this headline interest or excite me enough to click through and look?

Imaginary Design.
http://www.imaginarydesign.co.uk/blog
The headlines on this branding and graphic design blog are succinct and descriptive.

Topic

I've just presented you with a list of blog article types that work, but that's just a starting point. Each time you blog, ask yourself: "Do I really care about this?" Great blog posts inspire others not just because they are entertaining or informative, but because the blogger is sharing something he or she cares about in their unique style. It has to come from the heart, and when it does your readers will feel a real connection.

Content

Remember that a blog post can be text, video, photo(s), audio—or any combination of these. If your main content is a photo or photos, make sure they are a good size. No one minds scrolling down to see photos if they are big and stunning. If you opt for a mainly written blog, do include a relevant photo, if you have a good one, as it breaks up the text and can enhance the message. I'll talk a little more about photos later in this chapter.

Length

My advice to bloggers is always to keep it short—250 words is plenty. If you are naturally verbose you might find this tricky, but it is good discipline. If it's 1,000 words long, it has to be a really great blog post to keep people reading all the way down. The exception to this could be a tutorial or recipe, or something broken up into steps. As you find your blogging voice, why not experiment—you might find the occasional "long post" is well received. Basically, brief and often is better than long and infrequent.

Readability

By this I mean things like a reasonably sized clear font in a dark color on a white or pale background, no background graphics beneath the copy, generous line spacing, short paragraphs and short sentences. These are all basic factors that can get overlooked. Your aim is to make it as easy as possible for people to read your blog posts, get the gist of it, comment, and subscribe.

White Lightning.
http://www.feelslikewhitelightning.com
Elizabeth Spiridakis writes her blog in her own distinctive and entertaining voice.

9/6/11

Obsessed With: Stine Goya

I bought this printed cotton **Stine Goya** dress-thing on the internets, sight unseen (it's basically the **Sassy** magazine pillowcase/dress DIY..it's a rectangle with holes for your body parts that need holes). It was a genius purchase.

It sorta has a rorschach print on it? As you can see here, where I am wearing it in from of a Warhol Rorschach. See? Rorschachs. (Ed Note: It is very pleasing to type that word).

It came with a fabric belt but guess what? SOmetiems I go rogue! Wear my own belt! Patent leather! YOU CAN'T STOP ME!

Ameesha Lee. http://ameeshalee.blogspot.com
Australian illustrator Ameesha Lee Earnshaw typically writes about 200 words per blog post, always accompanied by one or more photos or illustrations.

Links

Links between sites are the fuel of the web. Include links within your posts whenever relevant. For example, if you reference another site or article, make it into a link. You might also create a trackback from the link (for an explanation of trackbacks, see p. 112). If you are showcasing your work, include a link to your store or portfolio.

Social

If you want people to share your blog posts, offer lots of opportunities to do so and make it easy. For example, have "Tweet this," "Google+1," Facebook "like," or "Share this" buttons. (See Chapter 8 for more on this.)

EXPERT TIP: CHERI LUCAS

Blog: Writing through the Fog
http://writingthroughthefog.com
Started: 2009
Topic: Travel & Musings

"After two years of forcing myself inside a niche and restricting posts to what I thought 'travel writing' was, I decided to open up and write on themes that drive me on a deeply personal level. While the 'fog' in Writing Through the Fog suggests topics on San Francisco and regional travel, it implies something more: my evolving idea of home; the hazy concept of place in an increasingly virtual world. Readers have been very receptive to my looser focus, which allows me to experiment and fuse travel musings with memoir. The result? More honest, natural writing."

Credentials: Writer and editor Cheri Lucas muses and photographs her way through life. She has a BA in screenwriting from Loyola Marymount University and an MFA in creative nonfiction from Goucher College. Cheri is based in San Francisco, but hopes to embark on a travel adventure and find herself in southern Spain.

Mustard and Sage.
http://mustardandsage.wordpress.com
A clean, clear font and good line spacing make posts on this blog a delight to read on screen.

THE POWER OF PHOTOS

Ah, photos—every blog needs them, and they're so easy to come by these days, aren't they? Freely available on the web, easy to take using nothing more than a phone . . . but woaah! Wait a minute . . .

There is a minefield to negotiate here!

YES, visuals will be a key aspect of any creative blog, although if you're, say, an illustrator, you may find you use very few photos.

YES, it's easy to copy images from the web, but most are copyrighted and stealing isn't your style, is it?

YES, smartphones make great cameras, but the photos you take may not be good enough, and you still need to be able to resize them and so forth.

But there's plenty of good news. There has never been a better time to start blogging—the bloggers of yesteryear had many problems to contend with, not least of all slow processor speeds and painfully slow internet connections. This meant that if you used too many photos on a web page the whole thing froze or refused to load. There is a big choice of inexpensive digital cameras on the market now, many free photo manipulation tools, and a huge amount of free information on the web for anyone interested in learning how to use them. So, let's now look at the basic considerations for using photos on your blog.

Simone Walsh.
http://www.blog.simonewalsh.com
People love a story in pictures, such as Simone Walsh's post "Progress on my new jewellery studio."

50mm. http://blog.50mm.jp
Japan-based photographer Sean Wood calls his blog a "personal notepad" for the various tests and experiments he's working on.

Selecting photos for your blog

By far the best way of getting photos for your blog is to take your own. That way, you can get exactly the shot you want, you're not beholden to someone else's style, there will be a consistency throughout your blog, and, best of all, you own the copyright to the images. If you don't have any photography skills then it might be worth getting some tuition and investing in a decent digital camera. You don't have to spend a fortune but if you want to create fantastic, beautiful images of your work then it's worth it. If you are more of a verbal than visual creative, for example an author, poet, or journalist, you may not feel the need to take your own photos, or you may decide that your phone camera is sufficient.

An alternative to taking your own photos is to use a royalty-free image library such as iStockphoto.com. You pay a licence fee per image, ranging from a few dollars to several hundred. Or you could search a community site like Flickr.com and approach individual photographers for permission to use their work. Some are happy for you to do so under a Creative Commons Licence in return for a credit.

Something to think about is quality. In print, photos need to be high resolution, or "high res," which means a minimum 300 dots per inch (dpi), otherwise they appear grainy. But on the web, 150 dpi or even 70 dpi (low resolution) can be sufficient for the image to display crisply. Another reason to avoid copying images from the web is that they are likely to be already low res, and probably quite small, whereas if you start with a large, high res image you can resize without any loss of quality.

Also, bear in mind that an image that has been compressed, such as one with the file ending .jpg, can certainly be made smaller, but it cannot be made bigger just by changing the dimensions—the quality will be very poor.

Photo editing

Once you have the photos you want to use, it's unlikely that you can just upload them right away. For example they may be too big, too high resolution, too dark, the wrong shape, or you might just want to use part of the image. You need to be able to do at least some basic editing of images.

Professional designers and artists use image-manipulation software such as Adobe Photoshop, but if you're only needing to edit images for your blog it's unlikely you will need industry-standard stuff. The most basic functions you need are cropping and resizing, but you may also want to be able to lighten or darken an image, or apply the odd effect.

Your computer should have an image editor already installed—Microsoft Paint if you're using a PC and iPhoto if you are on a Mac. At the time of writing Google's Picnik was due to be shutdown, but check out Google+ which is set to include a photo-editing tool. A step up from this might be Adobe Photoshop Elements, which although not free, is a fraction of the cost of Photoshop.

Using photos on your blog

I've mentioned before that bigger images are more eye-catching, and you may opt to make your photos the full width of a column. Experiment to see how smaller images look: try "floating" them left or right around text, or leaving white space around them. When you resize an image, the relative dimensions will be retained, unless you specify otherwise. When you crop, it's up to you. Play around with your photo-editing software and see what you can achieve.

NEED TO KNOW: PHOTO FILE FORMATS

The file formats for photos that you may come across are .jpg, .png, and .tif. The most commonly supported on blogs is .jpg. Tif files are larger, so make sure you save any .tif images as .jpg using your photo-editing software. The file ending .gif is best used only for line drawings or single-color images rather than full-color photos.

iPhoto

If you're working on a Mac, it comes with iPhoto, an excellent free tool for editing your photos, making it very easy to crop, resize, adjust color and brightness, and many other effects.

EXPERT TIP: **LAURA TREVEY**

Blog: Bright, Bold & Beautiful
http://brightboldbeautiful.blogspot.com
Started: 2009
Topic: Art, Design & Fashion

"People often ask me, 'What is a blog?' For me, a blog is an online magazine, so it must be visually stunning. I would say make sure every post has at least one photo. Invest in a good camera, and take good quality photos!"

Credentials: Laura Trevey's first blog was designed to attract viewers to her online watercolor shop. But she immediately fell in love with the whole concept of blogging and after six months started Bright, Bold & Beautiful. The blog features not only Laura's work but also what inspires her, in particular beautiful interiors, fashion, and design. Laura is the author of *smART Business*, a practical and visually exciting how-to book for artists and crafters.

Many great creative blogs use lots of images per post. This can be very impactful, but beware that it might make your blog load rather slowly for some people. If your blog posts are going to be long and comprised of many photos, consider limiting the number of posts displaying per page. (You can do this in your blog's settings.)

When you upload a photo, remember to tag it with keywords. These will make the image easier to find not only when someone searches your site but also in web engine searches.

Protecting your copyright

Sorry to break it to you, but there's no foolproof way of protecting your work once it's on the web. If someone is determined enough they will use your images. Brands spend huge amounts of money on detecting breaches of copyright and pursuing compensation. My advice is to put a copyright statement on your blog asking people to contact you for permission before using anything. With a bit of luck they will play nice and drop you an email. If you agree, they then give you a credit/link back and everyone is happy.

All The Mountains.
http://allthemountains.blogspot.com.
All the Mountains makes a big impact with large images and minimal text.

Fly. http://flygirlblog.com
Andrea Pippins started Fly as a daily resource to inspire young women to pursue their creative passions. Through video, text, and images, Fly reaches thousands of readers around the world.

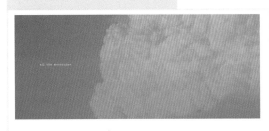

Proof from the wise and silver haired set that personal style advances with age

FRIDAY, SEPTEMBER 9, 2011

On Dressing Age Appropriate

Many people feel that women of a certain age shouldn't dress up, express themselves, wear bright colors, and even show a little skin. From my experience, the ladies I feature, feel more free to express themselves as they have gotten older. They care less about what other people think, and rely more on their own instinct. I asked a few of my favorite ladies how they feel about dressing "age appropriate", what an older woman should never wear, and if one can dress sexy as they age. Read their responses below and please comment with your own opinions.

EXPERT TIP: **JESSICA JONES**

Blog: How About Orange

http://www.howaboutorange.blogspot.com

Started: 2006

Topic: Craft & Design

"A common problem with photographs taken by non-pros and posted on blogs is that images are too dark. Dim photos are depressing; bright photos are inviting. Take a little time to edit your images and the look of your blog will improve."

Credentials: Jessica Jones is a graphic designer in the Chicago area. In addition to corporate identities and marketing collateral, her work includes a line of fabrics appearing on products in national stores and magazines. Jessica's blog, How About Orange, features DIY craft tutorials, free printables, and design inspiration from around the web.

VIDEO: AN ESSENTIAL TOOL FOR EVERY BLOGGER

If a picture is worth a thousand words then how about a moving picture? Even if you're more of a wordsmith than a visual artist, don't skip this section! On the other hand, if the idea of writing all your blog posts takes you back to the tenth grade and homework assignments, relax. Video blogging (sometimes called vlogging) is an established alternative to the written word, and it's as accessible as it has ever been.

Video blogging doesn't mean all your blog posts have to be shot on video. But here are some compelling reasons why you should seriously think about including video content on your blog.

People love to watch video
In 2009, around 85% of the total US internet audience viewed online video. Many bloggers report that their video content receives consistently higher viewing figures and comments than written blog posts.

Video is social
There's something about seeing a person on screen rather than just reading their words that creates a connection. This in turn can encourage people to make contact with you as they feel they already "know" you a little. Good video content often gets shared on social networks; it's a big driver of social media.

Video shows, rather than tells
Got something to explain to your audience but struggling to write it out in "how-to" steps? Being able to watch a process as it happens, or see what you mean exactly by "tap gently into place" or "insert the needle from left to right through the front of the first stitch" is very powerful.

iMovie
On a Mac, editing and exporting your video is straightforward in iMovie.

The Art of Photography.
The Art of Photography is a popular weekly video podcast dedicated to discussing all things photography related.

Video can be done cheaply

There's no need to spend a fortune on equipment. Many bloggers use the video camera function on their phone or a pocket video camcorder to shoot footage, and both PCs and Macs come with free video-editing software.

Video content helps grow your blog audience

Your video content stands a great chance of being found in searches, especially if you tag it with keywords. As well as displaying on your blog, if hosted at YouTube or Facebook your video will attract new people to your blog.

Blogs typically make use of short format video. But if video is your thing, you might progress to video podcasting, which is a little more ambitious. We'll look at podcasting later in this chapter.

Crochet Mania.
http://crochet-mania.blogspot.com
Teresa Richardson creates crochet tutorials which she hosts on YouTube and embeds at Crochet Mania, one of her several blogs.

Beginner Crochet Stitches and Techniques

EXPERT TIP: **DAN BLANK**

Blog: We Grow Media	
http://wegrowmedia.com	
Started: 2009	
Topic: Publishing	

"Twice a week, I post long-form video interviews with those in publishing who inspire me. Posting these videos brings me closer to those I admire, and my audience closer to them as well. I have also found that the more I share of myself, the more people connect with me in return. In an age where we are all becoming 'brands,' there is something powerful in being human."

Credentials: After a decade as Director of Content Strategy & Development for Reed Business Information, Dan Blank founded We Grow Media as a resource for writers and publishers. A regular speaker at conferences, Dan has trained hundreds of writers to grow their online content and marketing skills and to build their author platform. He also works with publishers of all kinds.

STEP-BY-STEP: MAKE A VIDEO

Creating and posting video to your blog is easy. Video blog posts are best kept short—two minutes or less is good. That way you will keep people's attention. You can always break down a longer video into shorter sections and make it into a series.

1. Lights, camera . . .

If you have video on your cell phone then you're already up and running! Alternatively, go get yourself a budget pocket video camcorder such as a Flip. Although the Flip went out of production in 2011, there are still plenty around and you could pick up a bargain. You don't need anything fancier that this when you're starting out, and unless you're a budding filmmaker you might even stick with it for some time. Many vloggers also use their computer's webcam to record simple "talking head" blog posts to camera.

Garden Fork. http://www.gardenfork.tv
Eric Gunnar Rochow started a video podcast about "cooking, gardening, and other fun stuff," and before long he had a hugely popular show on his hands.

TAKE IT FURTHER
Getting More Professional Results From Your Video
When you outgrow budget video production, or if filming is your thing, you will want to upgrade to a better camera with more features. An external microphone will give you far clearer sound recording and a tripod is a must. When it comes to editing, again there are a number of good semi-professional software programs to choose from, just make sure what you opt for is compatible with your camera and the computer you will be editing on.

The market for camera equipment and video-editing software is huge and the different media, formats, and features can be confusing. Do your research: there are plenty of sites where you will find advice. Try eHow.com and videojug.com for starters.

2. Action!

Before you start filming, plan where and what you want to cover and work out at least a basic script. Once you have that, just as with most things, you'll only get better at video by practicing, so go for it! It's worth remembering that good lighting will help make your video look more professional—indoors is tricky, so shoot in good, natural light if you can. Also, the built-in microphone in a budget cam won't cope well with noisy environments, so find somewhere quiet if you can.

3. Edit your video

You may need to shoot half an hour of footage to get a short two-minute video you're happy with. Windows Movie Maker is free editing software for a PC, and on a Mac you'll have iMovie. I would recommend these when you're starting out as they are easy to use and have lots of ready-made effects. You shouldn't have a problem transferring video footage from your cell phone or pocket camcorder, but having said that, do check with the manufacturer's instructions. You'll find plenty of online tutorials and forums to help you.

4. Upload & publish

If you have a hosted blog at Tumblr or Blogger you can upload directly to your blog if you wish. You will need the Videopress plugin to do this on a WordPress.com site. A good alternative is to upload to a third-party site such as YouTube, Vimeo, or Viddler. Once your video is uploaded, find something called the "embed" code. This is the bit of code you need to publish your video on your blog.

We Grow Media. http://wegrowmedia.com /how-to-record-an-online-video-interview Dan Blank creates video chats for his blog, with both parties on webcam. The chats are displayed in a split screen format using FlowPlayer.

Pia Jane Bijkerk. http://blog.piajanebijkerk.com If your video catches the attention of other bloggers it may end up being shared many times over. For example, Naomie Ross's Letterpress video has been featured on numerous high profile sites, including the blog of international stylist, photographer, and author Pia Jane Bijkerk.

PODCASTING & AUDIO BLOGGING

As I mentioned earlier in this chapter, it's a great idea to vary the content mix of your blog. Video can really bring your work to life, but what about audio?

Now if you're a musician, this will have been your first thought. But audio isn't just music, of course: there is also the spoken word. You might imagine that audio is the poor relation of video and not that popular. But video did not kill the radio star—evidence surely that we love listening as much as watching!

Why audio?
- *When people hear your voice, it can create a deeper connection than just reading your words. It feels somehow more personal, particularly in the case of podcasts.*
- *If you're really not in the mood to write, or something strikes you as easier to talk than to write about, then why not record it? Remember those times when you've started composing an email or text, and you've given up and decided to call instead? Well, it's like that.*
- *Audio can create atmosphere and set the scene. Imagine a radio journalist reporting live from a carnival, or a concert, or the rainforest; ambient sound can add an amazing depth to your words.*
- *Audio is great for interviews and capturing someone's personality. And it's quicker to post the audio than to transcribe it.*
- *It's different! Throw in an audio blog post every now and again and your blog subscribers are sure to notice and comment.*

How to put audio content on your blog

As with video, it costs virtually nothing to create a basic recording on your computer. But, similarly, you can spend plenty on recording equipment and software —it's up to you. Mac users can make a spoken recording using their computer's built-in microphone, and edit it in Garageband. If you are on a PC, you may need to install some free software such as Audacity. An external microphone is a good idea though, and they are not expensive. For something quick and easy, you can record and post audio content from a smartphone. For example, using a service called Audioboo (http://audioboo.fm).

Save your audio recording as an MP3 file. You can either upload it to your blog (which may incur a cost for the extra storage space), or host it elsewhere and embed the file, much as you would do with video. For example, if your blog is hosted at WordPress.com you can upload your audio if you purchase a space upgrade. Or, you could sign up for a service such as SoundCloud or ReverbNation (http://www.reverbnation.com) where you can host your audio files, customize how they look when they are embedded on your blog, and monitor the statistics of who has listened to your audio. There are many options for this, so do a little investigation on the web and you will find something that suits you.

SoundCloud. http://soundcloud.com
LA Foodie. http://lafoodie.com
SoundCloud is an audio hosting service used by thousands of musicians
and bands, and you can also host podcasts there, as do LA Foodie.

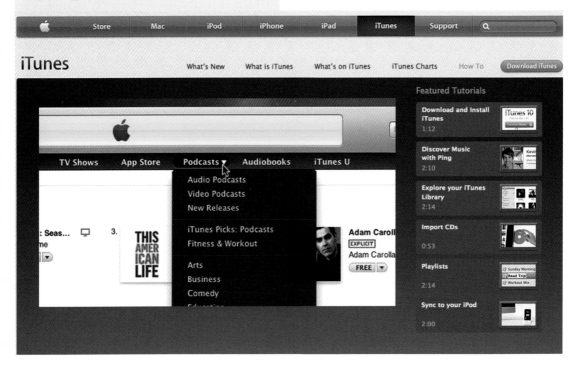

iTunes. http://www.apple.com/itunes
Go to Apple's iTunes pages to find out all about creating, submitting, and discovering podcasts. There are more than 100,000 audio and video podcasts in its directory.

Create a podcast!

If you really get into audio content, you might even consider podcasting, although it's a much bigger commitment than just posting the odd short snippet on your blog. An audio podcast is a chunk of audio content that subscribers can download and listen to later—which can mean away from the web; all you need to listen to a podcast is a computer or an MP3 player. Although podcasting gets its name from the Apple iPod, you don't need an Apple device. In fact, nowadays many cell phones incorporate MP3 players.

Rather then it being a one-off, a podcast is generally a regular event, like a radio show (or a TV show—you can also make video podcasts). When you record an episode, you need to upload it to a podcast host such as Podbean, then submit it to podcast directories (the biggest being iTunes) where your prospective listeners will find it and subscribe to it. This means that each time your listeners open up iTunes, any new episodes of your podcast will be automatically downloaded to their computer or handheld device. It's just like opening up Google Feed Reader and seeing all the latest posts from the blogs you subscribe to. In fact, it uses the same technology, called RSS.

Microphones

You can record audio content using your computer's built in microphone, but sound quality will be better if you use an external mic.

NEED TO KNOW:
WHAT IS A FEED READER?

Every blog or podcast has its own feed (also called RSS feed, or just RSS), which can be accessed via a feed reader (or RSS reader). This is the software that "grabs" feeds from the sites you have subscribed to and displays them in a format ready to read. Popular feed readers are Google Reader, Feedlooks, and Newsgator. Think of a feed reader as being like Outlook, Gmail, or any other email client. An email client collects up all your emails in one place for you to read them; a feed reader does the same for your feeds.

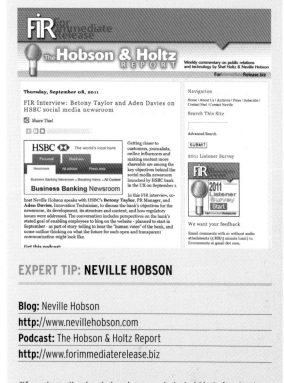

EXPERT TIP: NEVILLE HOBSON

Blog: Neville Hobson
http://www.nevillehobson.com
Podcast: The Hobson & Holtz Report
http://www.forimmediaterelease.biz

"If you haven't yet got clear in your mind what kind of podcast you want to do—or even if you already have an idea for what you want to do—take a little time to explore the iTunes podcast directory as well as Audioboo. On iTunes, you'll find thousands of podcast episodes. Look for some in the broad topic category or genre you're interested in. Subscribe to a few; that will give you ideas. The same goes for Audioboo. Like all things with social media: listen before you speak."

Credentials: Neville Hobson is a leading communicator, blogger, and podcaster. He co-presents The Hobson & Holtz Report, a weekly business podcast he started with Shel Holtz in 2005 that addresses the intersection of business, communication, and technology. Neville is in demand as a speaker and consultant. He is a founding Senior Research Fellow and Advisory Board member of the Society for New Communications Research, a non-profit think tank.

CREATING YOUR CONTENT PLAN

You've got the ideas for some great blog posts, you've started blogging, but for many bloggers the hard part is keeping the momentum going. The answer is to have a content plan. There's no hard and fast rule about the form your plan should take. Here are the kinds of things that work for others and might work for you.

Firstly, decide how often you plan to post to your blog. Be realistic about how much time you have for blogging, how fast-changing your area of interest is, and how often you will have new material to blog about. Your posting frequency need not be set in stone, but it's better to post at roughly regular intervals. If you blog in intensive bursts with long silent intervals in between, readers won't know what's going on and may lose interest.

Design Milk.
http://design-milk.com
An editorial calendar can provide a useful content structure for your blog, such as this one at Design Milk.

EDITORIAL CALENDAR

We have a number of regular columns and features here or keep these on the schedule listed below. Use this form to **sug**

Deconstruction (once a month)
This column is usually from the perspective of by a designer, process of building or creating a specific product, whether it b product.

Designer Dailies (once a month)
This is a voyeuristic column typically from the intimate perspe owner. In it we follow them around for one day, expressed thro

Destination Design (once a month)
Here we find some of the best designy, boutique, unusual ar see, visit, and play).

Weekly (or monthly) planner

1. *Set aside some time before the start of the week, or month if you plan to blog just once or twice a week.*
2. *Create a calendar for that period—days/dates and times (if you plan to blog more than once a day), and highlight the days/times you are going to post something. This could be created on a spreadsheet or wallchart, for example.*
3. *Pencil in one or two topics. Look at the "blog post types that work" earlier in this chapter, to help you.*
4. *For each topic, make whatever notes you need so that when you look at it later you'll know what your idea was about.*
5. *As you do this, more ideas or follow-up posts may suggest themselves. You might want to make a note of these on the side, or on a list of future blog post ideas. Here is also where you can make a note of people you'd like to interview, photos or videos you need to make, or of other bloggers you want to reference.*
6. *Work through filling in the rest of the slots. By looking at the whole week or month on one calendar, you will be able to create some continuity and avoid duplication of topics or post types.*
7. *Having a regularly updated content plan like this is often enough, but if you know your time is going to be short and if you are "in the zone," you might want to create all or some of your blog posts in advance. You can still add photos or update the content before publishing your posts, or even after.*
8. *Next month, copy your calendar, change the dates, and start again with filling in content. Do not overwrite the previous sheet—that way you can quickly look back to see your blog topics from previous months. This is the way I like to do it, but of course, your blog has its own archive, which you can also use.*

The benefits of planning posts is that you don't have to wrack your brains for ideas later, when you might be too busy to think too hard about the blog. Get all the thinking done in one go, and you may find it stimulates your creative juices further. If something else comes up that you want to blog about, that's fine, it just means you have another blog post in hand for the future.

Regular features

In the publishing world it is common to have an annual features plan, and similarly you will often see regular features on blogs. Your content plan for each month could include one interview, one tutorial, and two "what I'm working on" posts, with one giveaway/contest, and a guest post every two months. Some regular features can and should be planned in advance—guest bloggers will need notice and giveaways take a little planning. Can you tie them in to seasonal events, industry shows, or family landmarks, for example? Even better.

The Strange Attractor.
http://thestrangeattractor.net
Regular features on The Strange Attractor include "Creative Couples, "a series of interviews with artists who are also life partners.

Creative Couples. An interview series about creative couples; exploring their work, experiences, and what they've found to love about working with their significant other.

EXPERT TIP: FERN RICHARDSON

Blog: Life on the Balcony
http://lifeonthebalcony.com
Started: 2008
Topic: Container gardening tips for apartment dwellers

"The best thing I ever did as far as blogging goes is to create an editorial calendar. Scheduling which posts would be published on specific days made it so much easier for me to post consistently and helped me save my topic ideas for when they were the most timely for my readers. My editorial calendar also came in handy when I was suffering from writers' block."

Credentials: Fern has been gardening in small spaces since the age of nine. Life on the Balcony is an award-winning blog about the container gardening tips and tricks she has picked up over the last few years of growing plants on tiny balconies and patios, and creating container gardens for clients. Although Fern is a qualified graphic designer and the holder of a law degree, her first love is gardening. She is a certified master gardener in Orange County, California, and a marketing manager for Kellogg Garden Products. Fern's book about small-space container gardening is due to be published in 2012.

BLOG CONTENT PLAN EXAMPLE:

TYPE	LIST	STORY	HOW TO	
OCTOBER				
03 OCT		How I made my own "poetry retreat"		
10 OCT	Three favorite nature poems			
17 OCT				
24 OCT			Poetry workshopping (ask Jo to contribute)	
31 OCT				
NOVEMBER				
07 NOV	My top three poetry magazines			
14 NOV			Approach magazines (get quotes from editors)	
21 NOV		How a particular poem came into being		
28 NOV	My three favorite new poets at the moment			

Here is a content plan I did for a new poetry blog, for its first two months. I chose a range of "blog post types" and decided to aim for two posts a week. Many of these posts can now be written in advance and slotted in. In creating this plan I also started thinking about new ideas for posts!

MY TAKE	REVIEW/INTERVIEW	ROUND UP	POEM
		Open mic poetry gigs in Sussex	
Are competitions essential for an emerging poet?			
	Pamphlet by a local poet		"Geography lesson"
	Ros Barber		
When I've used end-rhyme			Bonfire poem
	Tess Jolly		
		Online poetry websites	
			River Ouse poem
	John Agard		

CHAPTER SIX:
BLOGGING ON THE MOVE

The days of blogging where you have to sit in front of a computer screen are gone. As cell phone technology progresses, it becomes gradually easier to blog directly from your phone. I say gradually because there are still some barriers and limitations on mobile blogging (or "moblogging" as it is sometimes called).

Why would you blog from your phone?
There could be many reasons. How about:
- *You don't have a computer.*
- *You are rarely at the computer.*
- *Your best ideas/inspiration come when you are out and about.*
- *You take photos or video when you are out and about and would like to blog about them there and then.*

Start by looking at what equipment you have. You might think you need a smartphone or tablet in order to blog on the move, but you would be wrong. It is possible to maintain and post to a blog from an ordinary cell phone. Admittedly, you are somewhat limited, but people have been blogging in this way for some time. You probably won't want to type long posts on a cell phone, but for short updates, photos, and video (if your phone has that capability), mobile blogging is great. The services available tend to be social-media friendly, which means that you can automatically alert your social networks when you post something new.

Reckon. http://reckon.posterous.com
Poet, artist, and musician Chris Weige of Reckon has this Posterous blog as well as Tumblr and WordPress sites.

Blogging with apps
Download the app for your chosen blogging platform, such as WordPress, and blog on the move.

Blog by email

Can you send email from your phone? If yes, then you can email in your blog posts. All the major blog platforms support this: you are basically given a personalized email address to send your blog post to and it is then published for you. Most blog platforms (including WordPress and Tumblr) allow you to post images as well as text, and some give you the option to add tags to posts, so do check with your own provider as to what they offer.

Blog by cell phone app

If you're using a smartphone, download the app for your blogging software provider. You can then create posts and pages, add images, and moderate comments, all directly from your phone. You will still have the option of email.

If posting to your regular blog in this way doesn't appeal to you, or your blog platform doesn't quite offer what you need, there is an alternative: use a different blog platform, one that's more mobile-friendly such as Posterous (http://posterous.com), Typepad Micro (http://www.typepad.com/micro), or Tumblr. If your blog is already established and you don't want to move it or start again, no problem. Do what many bloggers have done already and run a parallel blog on a micro/mobile platform. This could be your "on the move" or occasional blog, complementing your main blog. There's no pressure to maintain a secondary blog in quite the same way, as long as you are posting regularly to your main blog.

EXPERT TIP: ROBERT MCINTOSH

Blog: Thirst for Wine
http://thirstforwine.co.uk
Started: 2009
Topic: Wine

"Timeliness is key to sharing a unique experience through social media (in my case, to do with wine). Posterous is brilliant for sharing content by email. Your individual Posterous email address is like a best friend. Simply send that friend your favorite photos, audio, videos, or messages, and Posterous shares this with the world, distributing it instantly to your social networks. Raise a glass to Posterous!"

Credentials: Robert McIntosh works in the UK wine trade as a Brand Ambassador, representing wineries from Rioja, Spain. He has been blogging about wine since June 2006 on the Wine Conversation (http://wineconversation.com), which looks at wine marketing, innovation, and culture. He has been blogging on Posterous since 2009, as well as across the social media landscape via Twitter, Google+, Facebook, Flickr, and more.

COOL TOOLS FOR MOBILE BLOGGING

If you have a smartphone, new blogging apps and services are being developed for you all the time: rather than just running through a list (which is constantly changing) I'd like to share with you some of my favourite tools, starting with Posterous.

Setting up and posting from your phone with Posterous

When I first came across Posterous I thought, "Wow, is that all there is to it?" Similar in many ways to Tumblr, it seems particularly good for posting photos, and connecting to social networks. It also has a community element whereby Posterous bloggers can follow each other. Posterous doesn't offer a great deal of functionality, which is probably why it's often used as a secondary blog, for blogging on the move.

Follow the steps below to create your first Posterous Space (an individual Posterous blog). To customize how it looks, login to Posterous on a computer and you'll see "Customize" on the top menu. From there you can choose from a range of themes. You can also change colors, add a header image, and change other aspects of its design. Don't forget to scroll to the bottom of the page to the "Save, I'm done!" button.

1. First, download Posterous for your phone.

2. You'll be asked to create an account with a username and password. Then tap to create your first post.

3. Type in your post, as you would an email. To add a photo or video, hit the "plus" sign. To add tags to your post, tap the "luggage tag" on the Title line.

4. If you have added any media to your post you will see an attachment icon with a red number. When you are ready, hit "send," and your blog post will be published.

5. Your blog post appears nicely formatted for a handheld device.

6. Your Posterous blog homepage displays as a neat list.

Other things to do now:

1. Set up your profile, with a headshot and a brief bio. Include a link to your main blog if this isn't it.

2. Go to the "Manage" tab, click on "Settings" and choose your comment settings.

3. If you would like to autopost to a social network such as Twitter, click on the "Autopost" tab to see the options.

Posting by email

Probably the simplest way to update your Posterous Space is by email. You simply send an email with any attachments to xxx@posterous.com (where "xxx" is your username) and your blog post magically appears.

The Posterous bookmarklet

Posterous has a "bookmarklet"—a button you can add to your browser's Bookmarks toolbar. Whenever you find a website, photo, blog post, or anything else on the web you'd like to post and share, you can do so by clicking on the Posterous bookmarklet. If you have enabled Autopost in your settings, this also makes it a very quick way to share stuff on Facebook or Twitter.

More cool mobile apps

Apps come and go, but three fun apps for mobile bloggers are Audioboo, Qik, and Instagram, and they've all been around a while.

Qik (http://qik.com) is a program for recording and sharing video on the move, as well as video chat. You can upload your videos straight to your YouTube channel or share them on your social networks.

Audioboo (http://audioboo.fm) allows you to record and publish short audio clips from your handheld device or the web. Audioboo has a Flash widget which you can embed (for example) into your blog sidebar, if your blog platform allows Flash. If not, there are other ways to do it—just ask the guys at Audioboo. At the time of writing Audioboo was free, but there was a length limitation. Plans are afoot to allow longer recordings and even podcast hosting.

A new kid on the blog is photo-editing and sharing app **Instagram** (http://instagr.am), which at the time of writing is only for the iPhone, although there is currently an Android version being developed.

CHAPTER SEVEN: PROMOTING YOUR BLOG

It's a big world out there. By the middle of 2011, there were an estimated 169 million blogs in existence, and new blogs being created at a rate of nearly 5,000 a day. So in that sense, you are not alone! But how does one grain of sand get noticed on a mile-long beach?

You will have your own reasons for blogging, and perhaps those are more to do with expressing yourself than taking over the world. But even so, a blog without an audience seems a great shame—so let's go get you one.

This chapter and the next are all about building up your blog readership. Old school promotional stuff, online know-how, and good old word of mouth all feature highly. I'll first be giving you tips for promoting your blog. Promotion is a one-way process, like most forms of 20th-century marketing—"we sell, you listen." It assumes a passive audience, who don't talk back. Now, if your hackles are up already, congratulations—your 21st-century credentials are showing! But don't worry, in Chapter 8 things will get a lot more social.

We are living through a time of not only great technological advances, but, as a result of this, also huge changes in the way we communicate; with each other, with corporations, with the mass media. Blogging is evolving new ways of doing things and as a blogger, you are helping to shape this new landscape. Grab the opportunity and enjoy!

A note about budget: there is plenty you can do to promote your blog, much of it free or almost free. But there is a cost: your time. Some bloggers find they really enjoy the "back office" jobs—tweaking the search engine optimization, finding directories and writing

Top Ten Lists
Getting featured in a "top ten" list, such as this one from Blogs.com (http://www.blogs.com), can be a real promotional boost. There is no reason why you shouldn't aim to achieve it!

blogs.com the **best** in blogs

BUSINESS   ENTERTAINMENT   NEWS & POLITICS   LIFE   TECHNOLOGY   TOP 10 LISTS
Hobbies   Fashion & Beauty   Food & Drink   Health & Fitness   Home & Garden   Parenting   Pets

guest top ten list   *by*
                                                          Shellie Goyal

Shellie Goyal is the founder of **CraftBits**, the original free craft project site that houses 1000's of free craft ideas. 3 years ago, she started **Craft Gossip**, a news and information site for all things crafty and which is managed by a growing army of independent editors. Shellie lives in Brisbane, Australia.

Craft Gossip's 10 Favorite Craft Blogs

Bakerella
Imagine making something that not only looks divine but tastes it too. This blog is sure to inspire you into the kitchen for some edible crafting delights.

Recent Posts from this Blog
- Check out the new bakerella.com
- Time to open presents
- Mini Maple Pancake Muffins

CraftFail
A close up look at when crafting goodness goes terribly wrong.

Recent Posts from this Blog
- Ice Cream Cupcakes... Nailed It
- Origami Nazgul
- Money Shot Lies, This is a Craft Fail

Cuteable
Looking for cute handmade finds? This blog is jam-packed with cute (as the name suggests) finds from around the Internet.

Recent Posts from this Blog
- Flickr Friday – part two
- Flickr Friday – part one
- Riot Raffle

Dollar Store Crafts
The global economy is no excuse to not do craft and this blog shows you just what you can do for pennies.

Recent Posts from this Blog
- Book Review: Fearless Fair Isle Knitting
- Redo a Pair of Flip Flops with Crocheted Granny Triangles
- Question: Trunk or Treat Theme?

Hostess with the Mostess
This blog is all about parties. It's not actually a craft site but it is filled with inspirational party ideas that will make your next DIY party the talk of the street.

Recent Posts from this Blog
- Friday Find: Cool Candy & Jewelry Molds
- Mickey Mouse Inspired Birthday Party
- Yo Ho, Yo Ho: A Pirate Birthday Playdate

Makes and Takes
A mix of craft, kids ideas and recipes - this blog has some fun realistic craft projects you can do at home.

Recent Posts from this Blog
- A Whole Lotta Books for an August Giveaway
- Milestone Birthday Countdown
- Rhubarb Crumb Bars

Not Martha
This blog has a fun name and lots of fun projects from craft, sewing and cooking.

Recent Posts from this Blog
- one picnic, three good ideas, two weird cookies
- links: food
- HP Project Runway challenge, episode 3: the one with stilts

One Pretty Thing

Recent Posts from this Blog
- Daily DIY

descriptions for them, maintaining your blog's profile, and so forth. But if you are blogging to support your business, or aiming to make a business out of your blog, don't forget to factor this in. At some point you may decide it's cheaper to spend money (whether it be on technical, professional, or administrative help, or on advertising, for example) rather than spending time.

Before we get into sales mode, one thing to note is this: you can't make a silk purse from a pig's ear. In other words, if the content of your blog doesn't interest and engage people, all your promotional efforts will be a waste. Start promoting your blog only after you have set it up properly, got it looking how you want, and started blogging. Focus on the content and it will build into the best promotional tool you could wish for.

A Bit of Sunshine.
http://rebekahgough.blogspot.com
Great content ideas are fabulous promotional tools, such as Rebekah Gough's "Ten on Ten" photo project, which she started on her blog in 2008.

EXPERT TIP: JAIME DERRINGER

Blog: Design Milk
http://design-milk.com
Started: 2006
Topic: Art & Design

"Art and design are my passion, so working on Design Milk every day is like a dream come true. However, I had many failures before (and during) Design Milk. By following your passion, even your failures are successes because they get you where you need to be.

"Running a successful blog is hard work. Don't let anyone tell you that it's easy or that you can make tons of money by doing practically nothing. In the early days, I spent my nights and weekends working on the blog while also working full-time. It took three years of doing that before I was able to quit my day job and feel secure. I still work more now than I did at my day job but the reward is that I'm doing something that I love."

Credentials: Jaime Derringer is founder and editor of the "Milk" network sites dedicated to modern design. Her flagship blog, Design Milk, has been featured in the *Los Angeles Times*, *Time Out New York*, *Singapore Home & Decor* magazine, and *Real Simple* magazine. Design Milk is one of the Google Engineers' Staff Picks and a Twitter influencer in Art and Design.

GETTING VISITORS TO YOUR BLOG

Your blog is brand new and you want the world to follow it. Rest assured this is an ongoing challenge for almost all bloggers, unless you're, say, Lady Gaga.

To make the task a bit more manageable let's break it down into steps, and think about it in terms of what you want people to do:

Be aware of your blog's existence

Visit the blog and view something you've posted

Do something once they are there—such as comment, like, share, get in touch

Subscribe and become a regular reader

Obviously not everyone who hears about your blog will end up subscribing. A proportion of people will drop out at each step, often for reasons that are nothing to do with how good your blog is. Some people will subscribe and enjoy your blog without ever commenting, others may leave one-off comments or share a blog post or two without actually subscribing. To get people to even just view your blog you need to build awareness of it.

Cast your net wide

Who is your audience? The more niche your subject matter, in some ways, the easier it will be to raise awareness of your blog, because there is probably already an online community centered on your area of interest that you can make connections with.

But to begin with, you may have no idea how to reach that niche. So you have nothing to lose by casting your net wide. This strategy may well change once you start connecting with your audience. But to begin with, the more people that come across your blog, the more chance there is that a few of those people will be your future blog subscribers.

Tell your friends and ask for their help

Let family, friends, and, if you feel you can, colleagues know about your blog. Give them the web address, and (this bit is important) ask them to help you start building a readership by telling others about it. Rather than saying "please visit my blog, which is all about baking," refer people to something specific, such as a recipe you've just posted or a fun giveaway you're running. Announcing that you've started a blog is also a great excuse to get back in touch with people and letting them know what you're up to. A note of warning: be wary of blasting your contacts lists too often. Just because it is easy to send an email or update to all your

The results of a search for "recipe for chocolate cake" on Google, and the same search on Google Images. It's worth tagging all your photos to help search engines index them.

contacts, it is also easy to annoy people with endless promotional messages.

Sweat the small stuff

Put your blog address into your email signature, on your stationery, and onto your business card (if your blog is related to your business). If you don't have a business card, think about what you could hand out to people that would get them thinking and talking about your blog. It could be a conventional business card or perhaps something more individual or handmade. Or you could go one further and design a promotional decal sticker for your car! One thing you should definitely do is get a Google Sitemap for your blog, which will help get all your blog's pages indexed by Google. It's easy to do—see Google's help pages or those of your blog host for details.

Start thinking "search"

If the research is to be believed, there are two things everyone is doing on the internet: searching the web and social networking (including things like playing games). It's what online marketers talk about all the time: search and social. Now blogging is inherently social, as we shall see particularly in the next chapter, but not all blogs get found in searches. So the sooner you start thinking "search," the better!

The good news is that the more frequently you update your blog, the more Google will love you. Search engines are looking to serve up fresh, relevant content in their search results pages (SERPs). To help them find you, make sure you tag your blog posts with relevant keywords—the words or phrases that people are likely to be searching for. Make sure all your content is tagged, including photos, audio, and video.

SEO Book. http://www.seobook.com
There is plenty of information on the web about how to do SEO yourself, if you'd like to find out more. For example, check out SEO Book.

There are other things you can do to help ensure your blog posts get found on the web, such as:

1. *If your blog host provides Search Engine Optimization (SEO) support then you should be able to write the Title and Description for each blog post. Alternatively you may need to find a plugin for this. Search engines pay attention to page Titles, so make sure the Title includes your keyword or phrase for that blog post. Here is how the Title and Description of blog The Post Family (http://www.thepostfamily. com) look in the source code of the page:*

```
<title>The Post Family</title>
<meta name="description" content="The
Post Family is an Art &amp; Design
Collective, Blog, Gallery, Store and
Website from Chicago." />
```

2. Adjust your blog settings so that new posts are given meaningful URLs, rather than numbers, which mean nothing to search engines. For example, http://www.regencycostumeblog.com/how_to_make_a_regency_bonnet.html is better than http://www.regencycostumeblog.com/10_24_2011_789246.html

3. Develop some good in-bound links to your blog. This will be a long-term, ongoing activity and although there are low cost tools and services available on the web (Google "link building" and you will see what I mean), by far the best way of doing this is the hard way, which I'm going to talk about next.

TAKE IT FURTHER:
SEARCH ENGINE OPTIMIZATION (SEO)

In a nutshell, SEO is the art and science of getting web pages found on the first page of search engine results. It is a huge industry. Practitioners range from those who do it via legitimate methods (so-called "white hat" techniques) to the murky world of "black hats" who will do anything to game the search rankings. There are also plenty of shades of gray in between! Needless to say, all techniques described in this book are white hat. However, search engines change their algorithms (the way that rankings are calculated) almost daily, so if you want to keep up then subscribe to a blog such as http://searchenginewatch.com.

EXPERT TIP: SAMANTHA MCARTHUR

Blog: Savvy Marketers
http://www.savvymarketers.co.uk
Started: 2008
Topic: Online Marketing

"You need to find out what search terms people are actually searching for to help with the optimization of your blog posts—either to optimize posts you've written or to get ideas for new posts in your niche subject.

"The Google Adwords keyword research tool is a great place to start (type 'Google keywords tool' into Google and you'll find it). The more specific the key phrases, the better—no single word keywords, it's key phrases you're after. You can also type a query using one of your key phrases into Google's search box and see what suggestions it gives you as you type."

Credentials: Samantha McArthur has been an internet marketing consultant for over ten years and helps small businesses get the most from their marketing efforts. She is the co-founder and a regular blogger for Savvy Marketers on subjects ranging from blogging to search engine optimization and social networking.

BUILDING LINKS

Links are what make the internet what it is—an enormous network of living connections. If you want your blog to be known about, visited, and loved, you need to link it to the throbbing mass of the internet.

You will come across phrases like "link love," "link juice," and "link bait"—they all refer to aspects of link building. It isn't a one-off process, it's something you will be involved in for the life of your blog.

A few things to start with:

- *There are inbound links (links to your blog from external web pages, sometimes called "backlinks"), outbound links (the other direction), and internal links (between pages on your blog).*
- *Not all links are equal. Some will bring you visitors, some will help others, some are to be avoided.*
- *Any visible elements on a web page can be made into a link (words or text, photos, buttons, video . . .)*

Link building is often undertaken purely for SEO purposes. If you have inbound links from web pages that Google has judged to be authoritative, then that will help your own status in the eyes of the search engine giant. But that's a simplification, because there are many other factors that can skew things. Nonetheless, link building has been seized upon as a way of improving a web page's search ranking, and is highly competitive.

Instead of focusing on the search engines, think of link building as a method of improving your blog's connections, profile, and reputation in the blogosphere. Long-term, you should find that good search rankings are a happy side effect.

How to ask for a link

If you want some genuine, good quality links to your site, there are no shortcuts. Yes, you can hire in "link building services" or buy a miracle tool that promises to generate thousands of links to your site and a torrent of visitors, but if it sounds too good to be true, well, you know where I'm going with this.

A good rule of thumb is to give before expecting to receive. That means linking to the people you're hoping will link to you, before approaching them.

Here's what not to do: email a high profile blogger (or leave a message on the "About us" page) saying, "Hi, great blog! I've also got a blog, at www.myblog.com, and would love it if you would add it to your blogroll, thanks!"

Instead: once you have identified a blog you would like a link from, start by subscribing to it and reading it.

NEED TO KNOW: WHAT IS A TRACKBACK?

A trackback is a way of letting a blogger know that you have commented on their post on your own blog. Let's say you spot a great blog post, and you want to comment, but you also want your own readers to see what you've said about it. So you post your comment as a blog post on your own blog, and you send a trackback. This appears in the comments list of the original blog post as a short extract with a link back to your post. Unfortunately, the various blogging platforms handle trackbacks differently, and some don't accept trackbacks at all. Trackbacks are another way of reaching out to and being noticed by other bloggers, but don't rely on them for SEO purposes because search engines often ignore them.

Feel free to contact me at any time, to -

- chat about you or me or capybaras or books or sea creatures or your favorite place to buy a sandwich or things that are filling the world with loveliness and swell-ness
- tell me about your creations
- tell me about someone else's creations
- get information about advertising
- ask me to take down something I've posted of yours (sorry! I just love your work!)
- ask me to collaborate on something
- send me a card or something! what's better than snail mail? not much. not much at all.

CONTACT

Submissions + General Inquiries:

Design*Sponge warmly welcomes submissions in the following areas: home furnishings and accessories, interior design (including personal homes), student design, craft projects and fine art, and graphic design. *We do not currently cover personal accessories, clothing, jewelry, or baby clothing/supplies as part of our daily content.*

At Design*Sponge we try our best to showcase fresh, original content. As such, priority is given to products and stories that have not yet been covered online. **Please indicate if your submission has already appeared online or been submitted elsewhere.**

CONTACT US

Contact Us

TCH stays relevant and fresh because we showcase content you do not always see elsewhere.

Conversely, this means that if you would like us to consider covering your product/idea/design on TCH, please submit high-resolution images with relevant factual information early. But if you plan to send the information at the same time to other sites and/or magazines/publications, please be aware that we will not cover it – *exclusivity* is what we are after.

If you know of anything cool we should know about, send us an email to bill@thecoolhunter.net

Before contacting a fellow blogger, always check out their "Contact" page. Popular bloggers receive many off-topic emails, so it is polite to at least look at what they have to say first. By showing that you've listened, you have more chance of a receiving a positive reply. These are extracts from the contact page of Where the Lovely Things Are (http://www.wherethelovelythingsare.com); Design*Sponge (http://www.designsponge.com); and The Cool Hunter (http://www.thecoolhunter.co.uk).

Leave a comment now and then. When you see something interesting, link to it from a blog post on your site, or talk about it and send a trackback (see Need to Know on opposite page). Add it to your Blogroll. Re-blog it, or tweet about it. When you do contact the blogger directly, let them know what it is you like about their blog, and maybe mention that you have referenced them before. Ask if there is anything you can do for them. But don't ask for a link, not at this stage. Think of it more as building a relationship first. If they visit your blog, or leave a comment, that's a good sign. If you then ask for a link, you'll have a better chance of getting a positive reply because they will know you a little.

GETTING LINKS FROM DIRECTORIES

Building up strong links with fellow bloggers is a slow process, but one that should be enjoyable as it will bring you into contact with all kinds of great people. It can be the start of new friendships and collaborations; new ideas and opportunities. But you should also try to get your blog listed at sites with a broader visitor base and high levels of traffic.

Alongside blogs, the web is home to numerous directories, portals, aggregator sites, and blog feed directories. Some of these sites will be businesses where you have to pay for inclusion, others more like community resources which may welcome content contributions or offers of help.

There are plenty of blog directories where you simply submit your blog feed. Just be careful that they are reputable—check out who else is on there—as some of them are scams. Some directory/listing sites will invite you to submit your blog for free, but you then pay if you want an enhanced listing (which means a more prominent position, longer description, photos, inclusion in more than one category, and so forth).

Finding good places that might link to your blog is part of the process called link building, which used to be an important aspect of search engine optimization (SEO) of a website. These days, quality is more important than quantity, so it is better that your blog appears on five relevant, high quality, well-trafficked sites than a hundred small fry "generalist" directories. Having said that, researching and getting good links can be hard work, but there are tools available to help such as LinkDex (http://www.linkdex.com), for example.

Alternatively, there are directories submissions services which can be a big time-saver. Just be aware that in outsourcing these kinds of tasks you are losing some control over where your blog URL appears. You are also generally charged per submission, and a submission does not guarantee inclusion.

Here are some blog directory/blog community sites to check out:

Technorati. http://technorati.com
Indexes over a million blogs and is probably the most famous and authoritative blog directory.

Blogged. http://www.blogged.com/directory
Easy to search by category and includes screenshots, user, and editor reviews.

BlogCatalog. http://www.blogcatalog.com
A human-edited social blog directory, which describes itself as "bringing bloggers and readers together."

EXPERT TIP: LISA LAM

Blog: U-Handbag

http://u-handbag.typepad.com

Started: 2005

Topic: Craft—Handbags

"I use my business blog to promote my products, give my customers an insight into who I am, provide tutorials (using my products), and showcase the bag-making skills of others. I believe the blog plays a big part in gaining the trust of customers. I hope it also encourages others to go into business themselves, as well as creating a little corner for us bag-makers to congregate."

Credentials: Lisa Lam is a craft book author and founder of U-Handbag, an online bag-making supplies shop for bag-making fanatics (and fanatics to be!). Although she runs a busy, vibrant blog, she says she spends most of her time "designing sewing patterns and kits, sourcing yummy fabrics, handles, patterns and metal thingamyjigs for bags, and book/magazine writing." And in doing so, she comments: "I feel I have truly found my calling!"

NEED TO KNOW: WHAT IS A BLOG FEED?

In the last chapter I mentioned RSS as being the delivery mechanism used by blogs and podcasts to push out updates. It is a signal that comes from a website (in this case, your blog) whenever you update it, which can be picked up by anyone with an RSS reader. The signal says there's something new to see on the blog. A blog feed simply adds some meat to the signal, either sending the entire blog post to the recipient's feed reader or an extract. Your blog's feed is not the same as its web address, so you need to find it from your blog control panel. Make a note of it—you will be adding to various blog directories.

GETTING OUT AND ABOUT: OFFLINE PROMOTION

Just because blogging is an online activity, that doesn't mean you can't use good old-fashioned "offline" methods of promoting your blog.

Attending events and conferences

This is a no-brainer—grab your business cards and hot-foot over to any gathering of likeminds. Tell people about your blog and be on the look out for fellow bloggers, potential collaborators, guest posters, and people who have been through the blog start-up process themselves to compare notes. Let the event organizers know about your blog, and offer to present at the next meeting on the subject of blogging for word-turners/knitters/artists/musicians (or whatever your specialty is). Plenty of people will be interested in what you've learned.

Holding blogger get-togethers

Once you've made contact with a few bloggers in your locality, why not hold a meet-up? Take photos, or better still do some quick informal video chats, and post them on your blog. Make a list of who attends and send them the link. They are bound to refer to it or post it on their own blog, so everyone will gain exposure to new audiences. You get a reputation for being a facilitator, and everyone enjoys an excuse to get out and socialize!

Visits with other bloggers

If you travel, make a point to meet up with a blogging buddy you admire and create something together that you can both blog about and use to promote each other. It's exciting to put real people to names and you're guaranteed to leave with inspiration and new ideas.

Giving talks

As I mentioned earlier, people love to learn and your blogging journey could well be a hot topic for all kinds of groups looking for speakers, from business networking groups to moms' coffee mornings; from arts festivals to industry events. If you're happy speaking to groups of people, this is a great way to extend your audience and help others too. You could end up on the national conference circuit—it's how many speakers began!

Helping out the press

The press are always on the lookout for great content. Rather than just sending out news releases to the local press about your blog's launch, why not offer something in return for a little publicity? More about this in Chapter 10!

Bluebird. http://bleubirdvintage.typepad.com
When Bleubird's "Miss" James visited San Francisco and met Erin of Calivintage, they got together for a very cute photoshoot.

Lost is a Place Too.
http://lostisaplacetoo.blogspot.com
Taking part in a local event can raise the profile of your blog. South African blogger Lauren Fowler was a guest speaker at a Creative Coffee Morning regular meet-up in Cape Town.

ABOUT ME

LAUREN FOWLER
CAPE TOWN, SOUTH
AFRICA

I'm an illustrator, knitter, graphic designer and thing maker!

VIEW MY COMPLETE PROFILE

VISIT MY WEBSITE

FOLLOW ME ON twitter
FOLLOW ME ON Pinterest

ORDER A CUSTOM HOOP

FOLLOWERS

So Many Things

I have so many things to say!
First off, sorry for not blogging. I'm still fighting to get internet at home. They don't like it when they can't do a credit check on you...

ANYWAY!

I'll be speaking at the Creative Coffee mornings event happening this Friday at Escape Cafe to kick off Cape Town Creative Week. You can check out the event and RSVP here if you'd like to come, or read more about it and my interview here.

Also, keep your eyes peeled for further developments at The Fringe Arts on Kloof shop, as we have something special for Creative Week.

EXPERT TIP: ALICIA DIRAGO

Blog: Dismount Creative
http://www.dismountcreative.com/blog
Started: 2010
Topic: DIY Fashion & Decor

"Build real-world relationships whenever possible. For many of us, communicating online is our comfort zone, but I've found that truly remarkable opportunities come up anytime I climb out from behind my computer to join someone I met on Twitter for coffee or attend a conference. Getting to know other bloggers and the people behind brands I adore can be fun and educational as well as energizing. I am a livewire when I get home from one of these meetings!"

Credentials: Alicia DiRago is a DIY, style, and design enthusiast. She currently resides in Houston, TX where she gave up a career in chemical engineering to start Dismount Creative, a company that offers social DIY classes that encourage women to Make It Fun, Make It Together, Make It Yourself! When she isn't teaching happy-hour craft classes (and enjoying the hoppiest beers she can find), Alicia writes a popular blog about DIY fashion, jewelry, and décor projects and inspiration at Dismount Creative.

EMAIL MARKETING

Long before blogs really took off, people were already self-publishing on the internet, via email. Although email newsletters are less talked about as a promotional tool, they are still amazingly cost-effective, especially for small businesses, non-profits, and bloggers.

There is a great choice of do-it-yourself, web-based email marketing service providers. It's a highly competitive arena, which means they are continually improving their software while keeping prices low. The other good news is that many of these email tools work beautifully with the major blogging platforms.

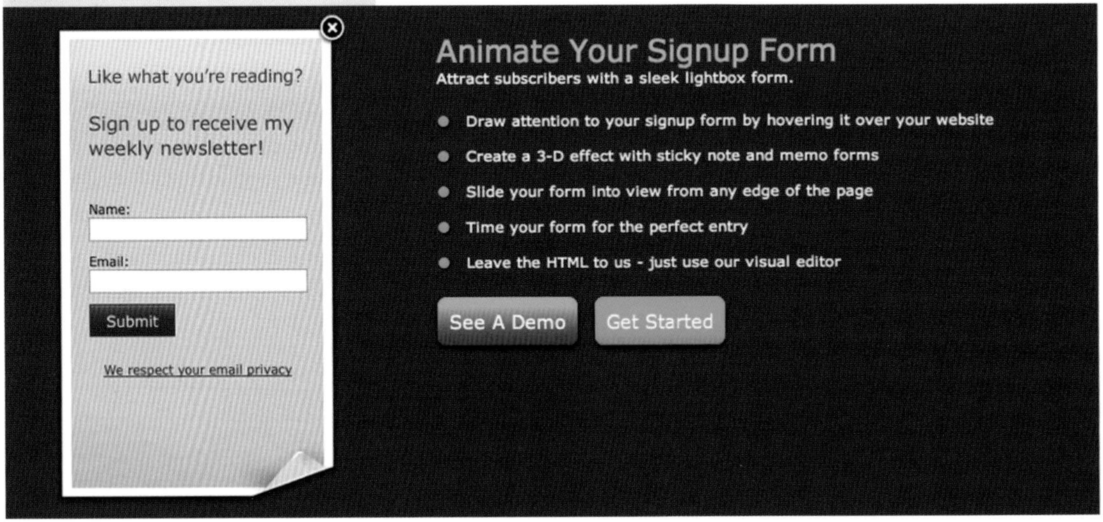

Why have an email list?
Won't people just subscribe to the blog?

It's possible for you to track how many people are subscribing to your blog (see Chapter 11 for details). But it's not so easy to then send them something by email as if they have subscribed by RSS then they won't have given you an email address. Also, even if they have subscribed to receive your blog by email, they haven't given you permission to email them with a newsletter, offers, or any other reason.

By asking your blog visitors to sign up for an email newsletter, however, you are building your own permission-based list. In this way you can "prod" your list occasionally to remind them what's happening on the blog, especially if you haven't posted for a while for whatever reason. Your list is independent of your blog and you can build it via multiple channels. In this way an email newsletter can complement the blog and help bring in new visitors. For example, how about featuring the following:

AWeber. http://www.aweber.com
AWeber offers a variety of form styles including a lightbox form that appears "on top" of your blog, until it is either filled in or dismissed. (This type of form can be irritating, but they do tend to improve the subscription rate.)

Like what you're reading?

Sign up to receive my weekly newsletter!

Name:

Email:

Submit

We respect your email privacy

Animate Your Signup Form
Attract subscribers with a sleek lightbox form.

- Draw attention to your signup form by hovering it over your website
- Create a 3-D effect with sticky note and memo forms
- Slide your form into view from any edge of the page
- Time your form for the perfect entry
- Leave the HTML to us - just use our visual editor

See A Demo   Get Started

MailChimp. http://mailchimp.com
MailChimp integrates easily with a number of blog platforms including Typepad and WordPress.

- a "behind-the-scenes" or "making of" story to go with a piece of artwork, video, or photo you recently blogged
- a featured blog post–this could be something from the archives which new subscribers won't have seen
- an incentive to forward the email or tell a friend about a current giveaway or competition you are running

Email runs quietly in the background, but many bloggers swear by the combination of blog plus email as the best way to grow readership and customers.

Putting an email sign-up on your blog

If you use a web-based, hosted email marketing service provider such as MailChimp (http://www.mailchimp.com), Constant Contact (http://www.constantcontact.com), or AWeber (http://www.aweber.com/), you can create sign-up forms and then embed them on your blog, maybe in a sidebar. Sometimes it involves creating the form in your email marketing account and pasting the code for it into your blog as a widget. Or there may be a "one-click" integration tool or plugin available to make the job even easier. Usually you can choose from different styles and customize the look of the form very easily.

Email newsletter tips

If you decide to sign up your blog visitors to an email list, here are few tips to help ensure its success:

1. Be clear to manage expectations on your sign-up form: what you will send, how often . . . and give people a good reason to subscribe.
2. Set up a "welcome" auto-response email to be sent to new sign-ups with a link to your blog and an invitation to subscribe to it. Maybe give away an interesting tidbit.
3. Stick to your mailing schedule.
4. Send at least every two months–any less frequently and people may have forgotten about you or their email address may even have changed.
5. Don't just duplicate content, or people will unsubscribe from one or the other. On the other hand, do sometimes recycle popular content from the blog onto the newsletter and vice versa.
6. Do use an online email marketing provider rather than just sending through your regular email client. Some of them are free to use if your list is small. They run on very powerful software allowing you to send beautiful-looking, personalized emails, track opens and clicks, and manage deliverability, unsubscribes, and bounces automatically.

CHAPTER EIGHT:
BEING SOCIAL

The web is social; it's all about people!

So your blog is getting known, you're promoting it like crazy and attracting visitors. Now let's look at getting those visitors to take action, whether it's commenting on a blog post, subscribing to your blog's feed, clicking on a link, recommending your blog to others, sharing a link, picking up the phone to call you . . .

Get the picture? A blog without evidence of people visiting is like a ghost town. But persuade a few folks to move in and kick out the tumbleweed, and before long you've got a thriving community.

The social web is here to stay, and if there's one guiding principle of the social web it is sharing and openness. This is sometimes a tough one for businesses motivated by profit and more comfortable with the idea of competition than collaboration. As a result, businesses have had to adjust the way they operate—not just the way they market—to take into account the expectations and attitudes of customers. Plenty still don't get this, but they will! If you are blogging for business, and if your blog is at the heart of your business, congratulations, you have made a great move. And if you are blogging for creative satisfaction, self-expression, to share your craft, expertise, or interest, or simply for fun, the social web is your natural habitat.

Social web expert Chris Brogan (http://www. chrisbrogan.com) puts blogging at the heart of a company's or an individual's online presence, calling it "homebase," from where you need to create "outposts" on the web. Outposts are things like a Twitter or

Sharethis. http://sharethis.com
AddThis. http://www.addthis.com
Here are two widgets for adding social buttons to your blog posts and pages. This is a convenient way to enable sharing, and you can monitor how many people click on the buttons.

Chris Brogan. http://www.chrisbrogan.com
Chris Brogan sets the standard in transparency and openness on his blog, giving full disclosure of all his afffiliations.

EXPERT TIP: JAMIE SCHLER

Blog: Life's A Feast

http://lifesafeast.blogspot.com

Started: 2008

Topic: Food

"Patience and confidence tempered by humility go a long way when building your blog community. Create a welcoming space (your blog), and one that reflects you and your personality, and highlights your talents; don't try to be an imitation of anyone else. Trust yourself and your instincts, and follow them, while gratefully accepting guidance, advice, and encouragement from those whom you respect."

Credentials: Jamie Schler is a freelance writer specializing in food and culture. An American living in Europe for 25 years, she is co-founder of From Plate to Page, an intensive, hands-on workshop dedicated to food writing, styling, and photography. Jamie has been published widely and her work appears regularly in *The Huffington Post*. She is an established food writing instructor and international conference speaker.

Facebook presence, a Google+, StumbleUpon, or Flickr account. There are thousands of potential outposts, it's a question of deciding what is appropriate for you.

In this chapter I will give you some pointers about establishing and managing your social web presence effectively, how to connect your blog to your online social networks, and how to encourage and nurture interaction. Blogging is inherently social, and your chosen blog platform is the first community worth exploring. All the bloggers I meet talk about how much they have learned from fellow Tumblr/Blogger/WordPress users and how generous others are in sharing information and creating new tools and widgets to enhance the blogging experience.

Before long you'll start to grow your blog community, become a valued member of one yourself, and have fun!

COMMENTING

As I mentioned in Chapter 2, one of the defining features of a blog is the ability for readers to react and join in the conversation. For the majority of blogs, this means commenting. There are some exceptions, for example Tumblr, which I'll come to in a moment.

You can look upon commenting in two ways: as a means to connect with people by starting or joining a conversation, or as a means to generate more traffic to your blog (the extreme of this being comment spam).

For most of us, the motivation to comment is somewhere on a spectrum between the two. It is natural to want to comment on other people's blogs, but there is no denying it also offers an opportunity to attract visits back to your own blog.

Commenting on other blogs

Your blogging action plan should include some time for visiting other blogs and leaving good comments. Start by going to Technorati, or Google Blog Search, and look for blogs in your area of interest. If you don't have time for regular "blog research" then at least keep your eyes open for any potential blogging buddies. Once you start finding blogs you enjoy, subscribe to them in a feed reader and read them regularly to keep up to date.

When you feel moved to do so, leave a comment. Being a good social citizen means helping people out and giving without asking for anything in return. A good comment will add value to the original post. In the blogosphere, leaving good comments will certainly make you friends and it will do your reputation oodles of good.

Some bloggers set themselves a weekly or monthly target for commenting, ensuring that they keep visiting other blogs and leaving comments on a regular basis. Regular commenting on blogs you enjoy won't feel like a chore, but I do advise setting aside an amount of time

Tatiana

It's great! Congratulations! The word is: PASSION!

AUG 23, 2011

svat

Trivial question, out of curiosity: Does the film mention James O. Clephane? (who financed and encouraged the invention of the machine, much as the supporters of the film are doing!)

AUG 24, 2011

Karen

We were at the Shelburne Museum in VT last fall. They have a replica of an old printshop there with a working letterpress. The also have a beautiful Linotype machine. I asked to see it demonstrated, but they said no one knew how to run it. I asked the docent if she could explain how it worked and she answered simply, "It's magic."

AUG 24, 2011

Ohmz

This sound really awesome. I want one!

AUG 29, 2011

Stewart

Nice film

AUG 30, 2011

and sticking to it, because your first duty is to your own blog and to producing great content for it.

What is a "good comment"?

- *Appropriate for the type of blog.*
- *On-topic, relevant. Not just "thanks, great post!" or "wOOt!"*
- *Not necessarily very long, just longer than one sentence.*
- *Accompanied by your name and photo (in other words, not anonymous).*
- *Polite and respectful.*
- *Part of the conversation, acknowledging other comments already made.*

Lobster & Swan.
http://blog.lobsterandswan.com
Lobster & Swan is the style and interiors blog of Jeska Hearne, where she shares everything from her "favorite recipes and decorating ideas to daily discoveries and inspiration." The blog has won numerous awards and attracts plenty of comments from loyal readers.

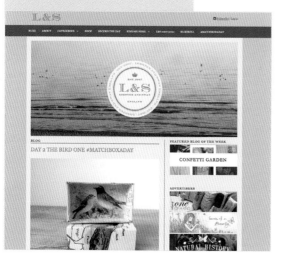

Commenting etiquette

- *If you leave a thoughtful comment, or a question, do go back again, because there may be further comments addressed to you. You can do this by checking "notify me of follow-up comments" or subscribing to the comments feed. "Drive-by" commenting, particularly when anonymous, can look as if you're not really interested in conversing.*
- *It goes without saying that you should use appropriate language and don't get sucked into "flame wars" (online arguments).*
- *If you are the blogger responding to various people's comments, it is polite but not obligatory to acknowledge each contribution with a reply of some kind. If someone leaves a really great comment, you could thank them publicly, for example on Twitter (with a link to the comment), or even ask them if they would like to write a guest post.*

NEED TO KNOW: WHAT ARE "NOFOLLOW" LINKS?

As I have mentioned before, when it comes to search engines, not all links carry equal weight. On a blog, links within the text of comments are generally "nofollow" links. This is a direction to search engine spiders not to follow the link. The idea is to prevent spammers from leaving links purely in order to help their site's search rankings. In practice, however, search engines make their own decisions how to handle "nofollow" links and some disregard the "nofollow" tag.

DISQUS

Robin Houghton (robinhoughton)

| Moderate | Tools | Settings | | Add-ons | Install |

Universal Code
WordPress
Blogger
Tumblr
Squarespace
MovableType
chi.mp
DokuWiki
Drupal
Joomla
Sandvox
Storytlr
TypePad
Yola

Blogger

1. Make sure that your blog is using Blogger Layouts. See upgrade instructions if not.

2. Enable commenting. See instructions to enable commenting. Make sure that **Who Can Comment?** is set to **Anyone**.

3. Click the button below to include Disqus in your blog. For best performance, make sure that the widget is in the bottom slot of the bottom-most right column. If there are multiple blogs under your Blogger account, be sure to pick the correct blog.

   (Add site "Robin Houghton" to Blogger)

4. If the widget does not work, please see this page for instructions to change your template to work with the widget.

5. Do you have existing comments in Blogger? You can import them into Disqus by visiting the import page under Tools.

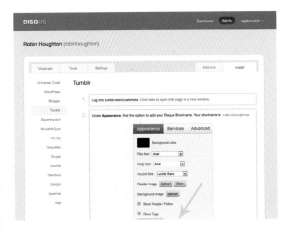

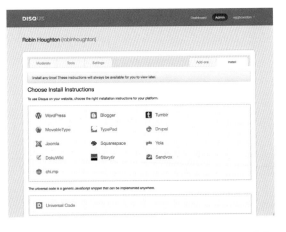

Managing comments on your blog

Most blog platforms include an inbuilt comments function. On some platforms, WordPress for example, you can turn commenting off for individual posts or pages. Your comment settings may allow you to do things like specify no anonymous posters, or set a "captcha" (one of those squigly, jumbled up images of a word) to try to keep out the automated spambots. Bear in mind that captchas are not foolproof, and as they are sometimes to difficult for even humans to read they can be a barrier to posting.

An alternative is to use a third-party comments plugin such as Disqus (http://www.disqus.com), which allows you to manage all your comments. It comes with many useful features, including things like being able to respond to a comment directly from email or from your smartphone, whitelist trusted commenters, and much more. Although Disqus started life as a humble software plugin, it has grown into a community in itself. But there are pros and cons, of course.

If many of your readers are likely to be on Facebook, you might consider installing Facebook Comments on your blog. This means that when someone comments, they have the option of cross-posting that comment to their Facebook profile. Their friends can then join the conversation, which appears both on Facebook and on your blog. There are both advantages and disadvantages to integrating Facebook with your blog, which I will come back to later in this chapter.

Another plugin worth mentioning at this point is CommentLuv (http://www.commentluv.com), principally for WordPress (but check it out—by the time you read this it may be cross-platform). If a blog has CommentLuv installed, when you leave a comment you are able to include a link in the footer to a recent post of your own. This is a great way of leading people to your blog content and has been shown to increase comments. One downside is that it can make your blog more attractive to spammers.

How to comment on Tumblr

Tumblr doesn't have a commenting function built-in, because it instead encourages re-blogging (distributing other Tumblr users' content) and "likes." You could, however, install Disqus on Tumblr if you wanted to allow people to leave comments.

Captcha
Some blog platforms allow you to set "captchas" on your blog posts to avoid comment spam.

To prevent spam, please type in the two words below.

(teoyome) raintour

Type the two words:
teoyome raintour

reCAPTCHA™
stop spam.
read books.

SEVEN WAYS TO GROW YOUR BLOG COMMUNITY (AND A QUIZ!)

We all know that money can't buy you love, and in the online world it's especially so. The author of *The Whuffie Factor*, Tara Hunt, talks about how social capital rather than money is the "capital of choice in online communities." In other words, be nice to people and it will come back to you.

How do you earn social capital and grow your blog community? I would say it is by being generous, helping others, treating people well, and enabling people to connect. It's about building relationships and listening more than talking—after all, everyone likes to be appreciated!

Here are some examples of what I mean. And since we're talking relationships . . . do you recognize the songs in the headings and the artists who sang them? (Answers on page 130!)

1. Oh won't you stay just a little bit longer?
When a new visitor finds your blog, after they have read that first post, what then? Think about ways of keeping them on your site by offering them something too tantalizing to ignore: a link to "part 2" or "latest update to this post;" a prominent sidebar widget with an eye-catching poll, contest, or giveaway ("only two days left to enter!"); or a short video clip promising something special. Surveys using heat maps (that measure how long people look at different areas of a web page) show how photographs of faces keep people's attention, so it could simply be through the addition of a photo.

2. I've been wandering round, but I still come back to you.
How will you encourage people to subscribe to your blog? First of all, make sure your sign-up box or call-to-action (for example "Subscribe now for weekly/daily design inspiration") is prominent. Even a small tweak, such as making the font size a little bigger or changing the color, can increase subscriptions. Another good idea is to offer a choice of subscribe method. Why not allow people to receive your blog by email, rather than RSS feed? This is easy to set up if you use a feed management service such as Google Feedburner (http://feedburner.google.com).

Mari Smith. http://www.marismith.com
Social media expert Mari Smith's homepage is full of calls to action, "teaser" boxes, and photos of her animated or smiling to draw you in.

I Suwannee. http://www.isuwannee.com
Although the options are there to subscribe by RSS, the email sign-up is fairly prominent on this blog.

Commercial bloggers use a whole array of tactics to get and keep subscribers, from pop-up boxes to piles of free information and offers ("value $5,289!"). However if you are reading this book I am assuming profit is not your sole motivation.

3. Lovin' you is easy 'cause you're beautiful.
Post good, original content. The number one attraction factor of blogs is the content, plain and simple, so post what you love, what inspires you, what you're proud of. Even though you may be showcasing or curating the work of others, having original content is vital and will be the X factor that sets your blog apart.

Fashion Photography Blog.
http://www.shionphotographyblog.com
The sign-up options on the Fashion Photography Blog are hard to miss.

Oodles of Doodles.
http://sschan.wordpress.com
Oodles of Doodles is a showcase for Sylvia Chan's illustrations.

4. Everything, all the time.

Post frequently. Time and again bloggers tell me that as soon as they up the number of times they blog, they get more visitors, more comments, and more activity on the blog. Many of the successful blogs featured in this book are updated daily or even more often than that. To begin with, you will be on a steep learning curve with your blog, so don't panic if you don't feel you have the time to post something every day. But set yourself targets—once a week is a modest goal. When you are comfortable with that, sneak in an extra post each month, and keep building from that.

5. You see I feel glad when you're glad, I feel sad when you're sad.

Everyone loves recognition. Whether you admire someone's creativity or are inspired by them, or just like them, find time and space for them on your blog. Help people out, without being asked—and the fact that they don't ask makes you even more prepared to help them, right? Always attribute stuff if it's not yours, and say thank you. Reward those who take the time to comment, re-blog, or like your posts. It doesn't have to be a strictly reciprocal thing (put us on your blogroll and we will do the same for you). It's just small things that let people know you're listening and recognizing the contribution of others in making your blog great.

6. 'Cause the world vision I see is the one—we for everybody, yeah.

Make sharing easy—I'll cover this in more detail over the page. But for now just remember to include share buttons on every post and page of your blog, and make the links to your own social accounts prominent. This encourages people to check you out and befriend you on other networks. Take a look also at Google Friend Connect, a neat social tool you can install on your blog as a sidebar widget.

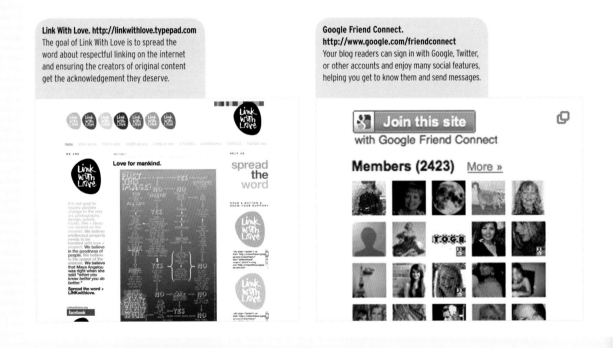

Link With Love. http://linkwithlove.typepad.com
The goal of Link With Love is to spread the word about respectful linking on the internet and ensuring the creators of original content get the acknowledgement they deserve.

Google Friend Connect.
http://www.google.com/friendconnect
Your blog readers can sign in with Google, Twitter, or other accounts and enjoy many social features, helping you get to know them and send messages.

7. Take off the mask, so I can see your face.

People connect with people, so show yourself—for example with a simple headshot or an introductory video. It doesn't have to be big budget or high production values (unless of course video is your thing) but it does have to be honest. Don't be afraid to show a little vulnerability in a blog post occasionally. You could ask for help, admit a weakness, or share something you've learned the hard way. Showing the real person or people behind a blog makes it unique and sets it apart from bland, corporate blogs. Give your blog a personality!

Chris Brogan. http://www.chrisbrogan.com
The "blogger's blogger" Chris Brogan is never afraid to show himself in his weekly video blogs and his open, honest manner is one reason why he has such a phenomenal following.

EXPERT TIP: DONNA PEAY

Blog: A Perfect Gray
http://www.aperfectgray.com
Started: 2009
Topic: Interior Decor

"The connections I have made with folks who have similar interests are, without a doubt, the best part of blogging. It's the daily conversations with my readers than mean the most to me."

Credentials: A beautiful blog that describes itself as "this girl's search for that one perfect gray wall color." The girl in question is Donna Peay and A Perfect Gray is a feast of interiors: decor, art, antiques, period homes . . . you'll never look at the color gray again in quite the same way! Although Donna has only been blogging for around two years, in that time she has been invited to New York for a television show taping and has had her blog included in a book about decor. She has also taken a writing position with a major home decor website. A Perfect Gray regularly receives 30-40 comments or more each post.

CONNECTING WITH FACEBOOK & TWITTER

Your blog may be your online home, but to get truly connected you will need to be present elsewhere on the web. That doesn't mean you have to be active everywhere, but you do need to find one or two social networks where you feel at home and are prepared to invest some time.

If you try to spread yourself too thinly you will spend too much time on this. The trick is to prioritize: never forget your homebase is your blog; do not neglect it! Let's look firstly at the Big Ones—Facebook and Twitter.

Facebook

Many bloggers create Facebook Pages (sometimes called Fan Pages or Business Pages) to support their blog. Having a Facebook Page can put your blog in front of a whole new, ready-made audience. Of course, it won't happen automatically—you will still need to promote your page within Facebook, but that's another topic altogether!

You will need a personal Facebook Profile before you can create a page for your blog. The beauty of having a page for your blog is that it separates the

activity of your friends and family from that of your blog readers or "fans." You may be quite happy to mix up the two audiences, but if you do decide to connect your blog to your personal profile, take care over your privacy settings.

There are plenty of bloggers who choose not to have a Facebook Page, not least of all because their blog takes up all of their time! Even so, you can still connect with Facebook by using "Share on Facebook" and "Like" buttons on your blog. They are easy to install and require no maintenance. If you find your blog is getting a lot of Facebook likes and shares, that may be the time to consider a Facebook Page.

Facebook is updating its functionality all the time, so you need to check out what's new. There are many good resources on the web to help you with setting up a Facebook Page for your blog or installing Facebook widgets. Online, check out http://www.allfacebook.com and http://www.marismith.com. Mari is a Facebook expert and well worth following for her excellent tips.

Twitter

If you only have time for one social network, you should seriously look at Twitter. Unlike Facebook, which is more of a tool to engage with people you already know, Twitter is more public and outward-facing. Someone once joked that "Facebook connects you with the people you went to school with, and Twitter connects you to the people you wish you had been to school with."

Twitter is sometimes called a "micro blogging" platform, because it consists basically of short updates —like a blog post only very short. You can post a photo, video, or link within your tweet, so "short" doesn't necessarily mean lacking in content.

So what's the attraction of Twitter for bloggers? One obvious one is that it takes up very little time.

**ANSWERS TO THE QUIZ
ON PREVIOUS PAGES:**

1. Stay - The Hollies
2. You're my Best Friend - Queen
3. Lovin' You - Minnie Riperton
4. Life in the Fast Lane - The Eagles
5. Can't Smile Without You - Barry Manilow
6. Positivity - Stevie Wonder
7. Behind the Mask - Michael Jackson

Confessions of a Cookbook Queen.
http://www.confessionsofacookbookqueen.com
Kristan Roland (aka the Cookbook Queen) is on Twitter and Facebook, and lets her blog readers know about it with a very cute set of social icons!

Whenever you update your blog, you can let people know by posting a tweet (and this can be automated, so no extra work). You can tweet from your mobile device; you don't need to be at a computer.

But it would be a great waste of the power of Twitter to use it purely as a promotional tool. See overleaf for examples of what you can do with Twitter.

Joe McNally. http://www.joemcnally.com/blog
Photo-journalist Joe McNally has amassed large followings on Twitter, Facebook, and YouTube. Check out the blog's wonderfully "social" sidebar.

Language of Light DVD
Learn More

Check out JOE's Books

JOE on FACEBOOK

JOE on YOUTUBE

JOE on KELBY TRAINING

JOE on TWITTER

- *Find and connect with other bloggers, journalists, and prospective readers of your blog.*
- *Have informal conversations with people off your blog.*
- *Research ideas for blog content.*
- *Help people out by answering questions.*
- *Discover things you never knew existed.*
- *Organize or take part in Twitter chats.*
- *Organize or take part in meetups ("tweetups").*
- *Show your personality and strengthen social ties.*

On your blog, create a "follow me on Twitter" button and add "Tweet this" buttons to blog posts to encourage people to connect with you there.

Thirst for Wine. http://tweets.thirstforwine.co.uk
Wine blogger Robert Mackintosh uses Twylah, a service which creates a branded "magazine" page of his tweets, organized by subject.

MANAGING YOUR SOCIAL MEDIA ACTIVITIES

So you've got your social presence established and there's the blog to update and a business to run and the family to attend to and Facebook comments to read . . . You also need to know what's working: whether anyone has tweeted your blog posts, subscribed to your blog, asked you a question . . .

Aagh! Are you getting that "internet overload" feeling? It's all very well my telling you to get out there and get social, but alongside having a real life, where do you find the time?

This is probably the question I hear the most. I wish I had the definitive answer, but it depends first of all on your priorities and your working style. Only you can make decisions about what's important to you, or how many hours to work; a book can't tell you that. However, help is at hand. An obvious thing to look at is time management. What's the most effective way to get everything covered? You will be pleased to hear that there are many, many tools available to help you monitor your social networking accounts, keep track of mentions, comments, messages, and trends, automate updates, and cross-post. And they are all free, or include a free option. Two of the most popular are TweetDeck and HootSuite.

TweetDeck. http://www.tweetdeck.com
TweetDeck allows you to customize feeds and schedule tweets among other things.

HootSuite. http://hootsuite.com
You can get HootSuite on your smartphone or iPad.

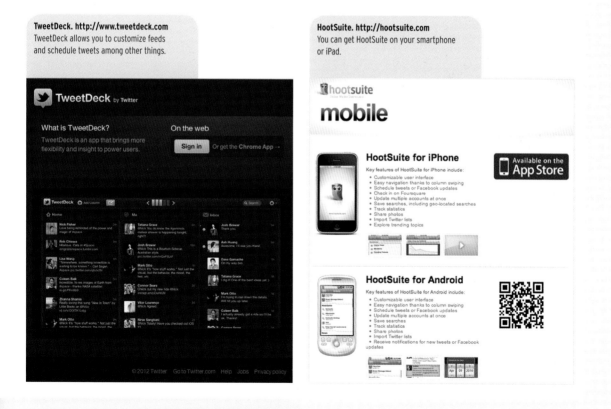

TweetDeck

TweetDeck is a kind of social media dashboard where you can organize and keep track of updates from those you follow, and post your own updates. Having everything in one place means you don't have to check the individual sites. TweetDeck comes as a desktop application for your computer, but you can also get it for your mobile devices. Since the majority of tweets are sent from cell phones, that's kind of essential.

This sort of tool can really reduce the amount of time you need to spend on social media activities: you can see everything in one place, and you can cut through the clutter of updates and make sure you don't miss anything important.

Let's say you follow 500 people on Twitter. Rather than seeing everyone's updates as a jumbled up, scrolling mass, you can create separate columns based on whatever criteria you wish. So, "Top Blog Buddies" might be one, "Local Friends" another, "Journalists/Influencers" another, and so on. If there are only ten people in a group, you're more likely to see their updates than if they were buried in the hosepipe of 500 followees.

There are many more features to TweetDeck, including keyword searches, tracking mentions of your name, and following threaded conversations.

TweetDeck. http://www.tweetdeck.com
It looks complicated, but TweetDeck is a great organizational tool where you can keep up with updates from Twitter, Facebook, LinkedIn, and other social networks.

HootSuite

Very similar to TweetDeck, HootSuite is a web-based application that has always been popular with social media consultants as it allows multiple users on an account (so consultants can co-manage accounts with their clients). If you are co-blogging with other people, particulary if they are based in another city or country, being able to share the dashboard, see what each other has posted, and co-manage the social profiles from one place is really useful. (The multi-user option is not free, however.)

The HootSuite dashboard fulfills the same functions as TweetDeck, with the addition of analytics (HootSuite has its own URL shortener owl.ly).

With a social monitoring dashboard at your fingertips, it can be mighty tempting to automate your updates and cross-post them to all your social networks at the same time. Just a word or two of caution: some kinds of updates can be scheduled in advance, and, just as with scheduling blog posts in advance, it's a great time-saver. But be aware that internet tools (especially when they are free) can be buggy and unpredictable, so don't rely too heavily on them always behaving as they should. And on the subject of cross-posting, be careful that you're not annoying people by sending out the same thing several times over. Be sensitive to the fact that your Twitter contacts may not be quite the same audience as your Facebook friends.

HootSuite. http://hootsuite.com
Using a tool like HootSuite means you can see who clicked on your tweeted links and other data.

HootSuite. http://hootsuite.com
Being able to follow the thread of conversations (as here, in HootSuite) is a great advantage.

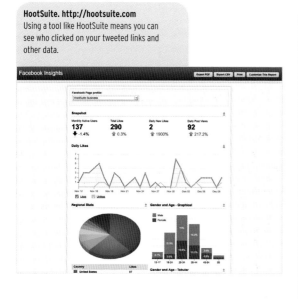

CONNECTING WITH OTHER SOCIAL NETWORKS

Whether or not you decide to make a second home for your blog on Facebook or Twitter, it's a good idea to have at least a minimal presence on a few of the major networking sites, even if you are not very active there. It just means you have a wider social "footprint" on the web: it creates more chances for your blog to be found in searches and more opportunities to connect with like-minded people.

What's a minimal presence?

An up-to-date profile is essential, otherwise it can look like an abandoned account. Fill in your profile as fully as you can and make a note of your login details, keeping a record of what you joined and when. Set alerts to remind you to visit/review at regular intervals—at least

every six months. (Believe me, I have learned this the hard way, signing up for things on a whim, then forgetting I even joined, let alone the username and password! If I were to start again, I would definitely be more organized about it.) If you do one thing, it should be to display your blog feed on your profile page, if possible. That way, people will see your latest blog posts, which is the main idea anyway. If you're unable to do that, just make sure you link prominently to your blog from your profile page.

Choosing where to hang your hat

It takes time to get the feel of a social network, and to decide whether or not it's your kind of place. I'm not suggesting you go crazy and sign up for all of the services

Fubiz. http://www.fubiz.net
The Vimeo channel of Fubiz, a daily blog about design, urban culture, products, trends, and digital arts.

mentioned here, but they are worth investigating. Ask other bloggers how they find them, and what other hangouts they suggest. It sometimes seems as if the social web is in a permanent state of flux—by the time you read this, there will be a number of cool new sites to check out, I guarantee.

Flickr

Flickr (http://www.flickr.com) has been around for a while and is probably the best-known free photo-sharing community. It allows you to store and sort your photos, license them for others to use, comment and receive comments on photos, and join interest groups. If you wanted to display your photos on your blog, you could install a sidebar widget that does just that, either as a series or in rotation. Flickr also allows you to upload short videos, but by far the most popular site for video is YouTube.

Other photo-sharing sites similar to Flickr include: Google's Picasa Web Albums (http://picasaweb.google.com) and PhotoBucket (http://photobucket.com), which are both free; SmugMug (http://www.smugmug.com) and 500px (http://500px.com), which have a growing community of fans, particularly among photographers, although they are not free.

YouTube

Often claimed to be the world's second-biggest search engine after Google, YouTube (http://youtube.com) has a mighty presence, even though there are many competitors for its throne. Reasons to choose YouTube as your video hub: the huge potential audience for your videos and the high visibility of YouTube in Google search results. YouTube allows you to create a channel for your videos and a homepage that can be customized, promoted, and developed into a mini-community of its own. Downsides include spammy comments and the

Patty Wormeck
Pinned 4 weeks ago from jensownroad.blogspot.com

Angel Food Cake & Strawberry Skewers

Rick Melissa French
Great summer BBQ desert treat

marinell guzman
Looks so delicious! i would like to pin this on my board at P.I.N.S.P.I.R.E. c.o.m?

this looks yummy !

Korrie Ford
Yum!

Deb Rimmey
Great idea

Pinned onto the board
Yummy Treats

Originally pinned by
Patty Wormeck

Pinned via pinmarklet from
jensownroad.blogspo..

5859 Repins

Victor Perez onto
For the Home

Becky Cogswell onto
Food

Ann McKeague onto
Favorite Places & Spaces

Amy Cranor onto
Recipes

Kelsey Dicken onto
yummm :)

Carmen Franchino onto
Recipes and Food Ideas

Kristie Hegarty Wilson onto
Recipes

Jenifer Lyn onto
my taste!

Lena Echevarria onto
Food I Need To Try (:

Rebecca Oliver onto
Yum!

+5848 more repins

fact that you are rubbing shoulders with all kinds of other material of questionable quality and taste.

Other free video-hosting communities: Vimeo (http://vimeo.com) is a favorite of designers and arthouse bloggers, while many pro bloggers favor Viddler (http://www.viddler.com), although you have to put up with ads on the free version.

Pinterest

It's been one of the fastest-growing social sites and as a creative blogger you will easily see its appeal, if you haven't discovered it already! Basically, Pinterest (http://pinterest.com) allows you to save, mark, classify, and store visual material you find online, via a special Pinterest bookmarklet that you install on your browser. You can also upload images from your computer. But that makes it sound pretty dry. The fun of Pinterest is in creating "boards" to which you "pin" any images that take your fancy; organizing them by theme, sharing them, and seeing what others have shared. It's like a social bookmarking site, but it's a bit more than that as you can really use your creativity.

The Pinterest community spirit is non-commercial, and businesses pushing their wares in an overly promotional way is frowned upon. But that doesn't mean you can't connect your Pinterest boards to your blog, your business, your Etsy store, or similar. As with all social communities, think about giving rather than taking: create unusual, visually interesting boards that others will want to share. Make sure that when people click on your pinned images they are sent to your blog where you give the recipe, for example, or tell the story of how you made it. Don't only show photos of your own work, but curate other people's material in with yours. Be sociable, comment, share, and have fun!

Naturally there are "follow me on Pinterest" buttons you can add to your blog, and on the Pinterest website there's a tool for you to create a "Pin it!" button so that others can pin your images as they browse your blog.

Pinterest. http://pinterest.com

Although still invitation-only, Pinterest really took off towards the end of 2011, growing from around half a million users to nearly 7 million in just six months.

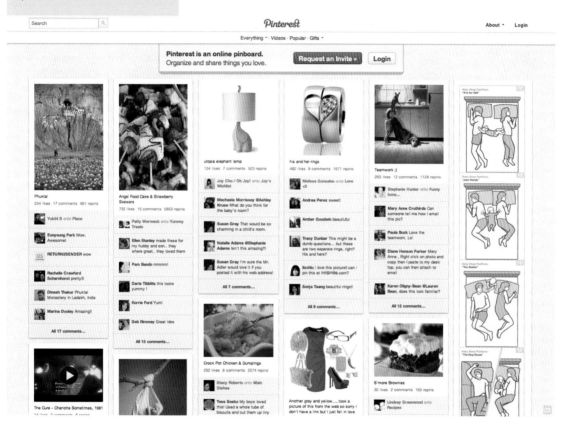

Pinterest has a "goodies" page where you can pick up buttons for your blog, install the bookmarklet and more. You can also get Pinterest as an iPhone app.

Chase Jarvis. http://blog.chasejarvis.com/blog
Photographer Chase Jarvis links from his blog to all his online hangouts including Google+ and his YouTube channel.

Google+

Google+ (http://plus.google.com) is Google's answer to Facebook and one of the newest additions to the Google toolbox. If you have a Google account, you can connect with others using Google+, segmenting your contacts into "circles" (so that not everything is shared with all your friends, as is the norm on Facebook). Other features include video chat ("hangouts") and customized feeds based on your interests ("sparks"). As with Facebook, on Google+ individuals have a personal profile, and businesses have pages.

When you create a new Google account, you will automatically be given a Google+ profile. This would suggest that Google+ is here to stay and its usage is likely to grow. Another recent development is that Picknik, the photo-editing tool acquired by Google, was shut down in April 2012, with the promise that it would be rolled into Google+.

And more . . .

I haven't yet mentioned LinkedIn (http://linkedin.com), even though it is massive. That's mainly because it's a professional networking site which you join as an individual. You can set up your blog feed to appear on your profile, but actively engaging on LinkedIn takes time and is centered on you, rather than your blog. Also worth a look is Blog Engage (http://www.blogengage.com), where you can submit your blog articles and have other bloggers comment and vote on them.

Of the many social bookmarking sites out there, check out StumbleUpon (http://www.stumbleupon.com). Think of it as a social search engine that makes customized suggestions, based on the ratings and reviews of its 15 million members. Encourage your blog readers to rate and share your content on a site like StumbleUpon, and it could mean your site getting suggested to others.

Bitly. http://bitly.com

Bitly is a tool for shortening, sharing, and tracking links. You can install it as a browser extension for Google Chrome.

NEED TO KNOW: URL SHORTENERS

A URL shortener is a little piece of code that converts a web page address, for example: http://news.bbc.co.uk/weather/forecast/2687?&search=lewes&itemsPerPage=10&region=world&area=Lewes into something very short, like this: http://bit.ly/dzSZCs. When someone clicks on the short link they are sent to the destination page via the URL shortener site, which allows each click to be analyzed. Using a shortened link makes sense when space is limited (for example, in a tweet) but it also allows links to be tracked and media performance measured. See Chapter 11 for more about this.

EXPERT TIP: JESSIE OLESON

Blog: CakeSpy
http://www.cakespy.com
Started: 2007
Topic: Cakes

"Once you've got some content on your site, start promoting yourself by creating a community–leave comments and get involved in the conversations on other blogs you like; submit your posts to sites like TasteSpotting and FoodGawke; promote them on sites like Reddit or StumbleUpon; link to your posts via Flickr photos (and join like-minded photo groups); and, of course, update Twitter and Facebook. If you're doing it right, fame and fortune will follow! Or not. But it's ok, because remember: YOU ARE HAVING FUN!"

Credentials: Jessie Oleson is a freelance writer and illustrator, and owner of the CakeSpy Shop in Seattle. Her writing appears on DailyCandy.com and Serious Eats, and she has illustrated for various companies including Microsoft, iPop, All-Mighty, and Taylored Expressions. Jessie's book CakeSpy Presents Sweet Treats for a Sugar-Filled Life was published in fall of 2011 by Sasquatch Books.

CHAPTER NINE:
HOW TO TURN BLOG VISITORS INTO CASH

It sounds great, doesn't it? Part-time blogger gives up the day job and turns professional, gets sent piles of freebies by companies, discovers how to earn a "passive income" from the blog, and spends the rest of his or her life on the beach . . .

It is worth starting this chapter with a tough reminder about the reality of blogging. We've all seen the websites and emails promising untold wealth and an easy lifestyle, all for the price of somebody's secret system or method. But if you're hoping to make millions overnight from blogging, you are bound to be disappointed. For the majority of bloggers, even for the high profile ones—no, let me correct that, especially for the high profile ones—success has come through a certain amount of luck and a ton of hard work. So, with that said, let's look on the bright side!

My Vintage Generation.
http://www.myvintagegeneration.com
The My Vintage Generation blog includes links to its Online Store and eBay listings in the menu bar, making it an easy transition for readers.

HOME   EBAY LISTINGS   ONLINE STORE   BLOG   CONTACT

Just My Type: A Book About Fonts

Published: October 10, 2011

I'm reading a fantastic new book about the history of fonts.
It's called *Just My Type* and is by Simon Garfield.

Many of us take for granted or don't realize the variety of fonts we confront in our everyday lives.
But, typeface can make an impact or generate feelings we may not realize.

SEARCH

To search, type and hit enter

SUBSCRIBE

 Syndicated RSS feed

CATEGORIES

> Art/Architecture
> Authors/Illustrators
> Clothing/Fashion

EXPERT TIP: CHRIS ZAWADA

Blog: Lovely Stationery & Lovely Package
http://lovelystationery.com & http://lovelypackage.com
Started: 2008 (Lovely Package) & 2011 (Lovely Stationery)
Topic: Stationery & Packaging

"Traffic, traffic, traffic: this is the key to monetizing your blog from an advertising standpoint. We started with Google Adsense on our site and as our traffic grew so did the checks that Google mailed out. Our issue was always that Google's ads are unsightly and detracted from the content we were publishing. A few years after we launched and our traffic grew substantially, we were approached by Carbon Ads which has suited us better."

Credentials: Chris Zawada is a Vancouver-based senior designer and art director. By day Chris works at TAXI Inc. where he provides strategic design solutions for a wide range of clients. By night he runs two blogs, Lovely Stationery and Lovely Package. In a short period of time, Lovely Package has become an industry standard for creatives and clients alike, with half a million visitors a month.

There are plenty of bloggers earning a good living from their blogs, and still more who may not be relying on their blog for their main income, but who make money from it nonetheless. There is no doubt it can be done.

The question to ask yourself, if you haven't already, is how important it is for you to make money from your blog. To help you decide, think about your answers to the following questions:

- *Do you need or expect your blog to generate an income, or would it be a pleasant side effect?*
- *Is the purpose of your blog not so much to do with making money directly, but more to attract people to your main business site or online shop?*
- *Is the idea of making money from your blog not important as you are blogging for other reasons?*

As the many expert opinions in this book confirm, the motivation to blog isn't always monetary, and even if it is, a blog can contribute in different ways to the success of an associated enterprise. Chapter 10, for example, looks at blogging as a PR tool. But for now, let's look at ways to generate a payback on your blog investment, both when starting out and as the blog grows.

AFFILIATE LINKING

You are the proud owner of a smart, beautiful blog. You're posting regularly, you have an editorial plan, and you're telling everyone you can about it. The blog is getting page views and some posts are being shared. But you don't have a big audience of regular readers. You're not the *New York Times*. Yet.

Nobody made serious money from a blog with a miniscule readership. But if you would like to test the idea of having advertising on your blog, it's worth looking at affiliate programs.

The affiliate model, in a nutshell

When you join an affiliate program you are provided with a choice of adverts (often refered to as the "ad creative") to place on your blog. (Where you place the ads is up to you.) Whenever someone clicks on the ad and makes a purchase, you are paid a commission. Sometimes you can earn a commission just for a click, regardless of whether it converts into a sale, but this "pay-per-click" model is less common.

In general, the publisher (that's you) receives no compensation for simply displaying the adverts.

Some affiliate programs are administered directly between the advertiser (or "merchant") and the publishers (affiliates). An example of this is Amazon, whose affiliate program is one of the longest running and most famous.

Amazon Associates program.
http://affiliate-program.amazon.com
The Amazon Associates program makes available a huge range of creative ads for affiliates to use on their sites, such as blog widgets to display slide shows, a favorites list, reviews, and more.

However, most merchants belong to affiliate networks, who not only provide the software on which the programs run, but also recruit affiliates, create ads, and manage the programs on the merchants' behalf. Joining a network enables you to find merchants whose offering best fits with your blog and your readers.

Making it work for you

Affiliate marketing is a revenue share model: you only earn money if your ads result in sales. Just slapping the odd advert in your blog's sidebar probably won't bring home the bacon. Successful affiliates work hard for the money. Here are five top tips for making it work:

1. *Choose your programs carefully. Are your blog readers really likely to be interested in this merchant's offering? Is it something you actually like and use, and are happy to endorse, even indirectly? Does the merchant or network offer a range of commissions and support or training, should you want it?*
2. *Select ad creative that fits with your blog. Ugly ads can ruin the visual effect and can look cheap.*
3. *Test, test, test—if ads aren't working, try different executions or different positions on the page. Just remember to only change one thing at a time, so that when an ad starts performing well you know why.*
4. *Don't just rely on display ads. Well-written reviews with links tend to have a better conversion rate.*
5. *Create some buzz. Get behind a specific product each month and theme a series of blog posts around it. Run a contest of some kind, get the affiliate link into your email newsletter if you have one, invite those who buy to do a guest review. Tweet about what's happening. Just make sure whatever you are promoting is something you really believe is great!*

A word of warning about disclosure: different countries have different rules about affiliate links. Some bloggers have a site-wide statement, explaining that the site contains affiliate links which are potential revenue-earners for the blogger. However, others will disclose affiliate links each time they are used, which in the US has been a Federal Trade Commission requirement since 2009. You should check what the law requires in your country.

Blog with Integrity.
http://www.blogwithintegrity.com
The Blog with Integrity pledge was created in 2009 to provide bloggers with a collective way to express their commitment to a simple code of blogging conduct, including disclosure of interests.

ADVERTISING & SPONSORSHIP

When you start considering how to make money from your blog, advertising is probably the first thing you think of. Somebody wants their marketing messages to appear in front of your blog readers, so they are prepared to pay for the privilege.

Having adverts on your blog is a serious step. It will alter the look and feel. Your readers may not like seeing ads. Ads take up space. And depending on the type of ads and how they are delivered, you may be accountable to advertisers.

One type of advertising popular with bloggers is Google AdSense (www.google.com/adsense). These are targeted adverts served by Google on behalf of advertisers. The ads that appear are selected by Google based on your site's content. In other words, they should be appropriate for visitors to your site. Basically, the way it works is that you earn a commission each time someone clicks on an ad shown on your site.

With Google AdSense, you have a certain amount of control over what ads are shown, and where they appear on the page depends on where you place the AdSense code. But you don't have the same flexibility as you would with affiliate links. Nevertheless, AdSense is easy to manage and for some bloggers it's pretty much a no-brainer. You don't have to deal with the advertisers or sell the space, and nobody will be asking you about your subscriber numbers or anything else to demonstrate the size of your audience.

One of the sticking points for creative bloggers can be that AdSense ads are a little ugly and there's not much you can do to blend them in with the aesthetics of your design. There are other ad serving networks however, one of the more unusual being Carbon (http://carbonads.net), a "premium, invite-only" service. Only one ad at a time appears on the publisher's page and the emphasis is on classy, well-designed ads from a small circle of high quality advertisers.

AdSense. http://www.google.com/adsense
Google AdSense provides walk-throughs and extensive help with setting up and managing your account.

IPAD DECÓR

PhotoMerchant - Create a pro photo website in 10min and start selling prints & digital files!
ads via **Carbon**

Photographic wallpapers based on travels & random outings by **Jorge Quinteros.**

All wallpapers cropped to 1024x1024 and scalable horizontal and vertical dimensions. Decorate your iPad.

HOME

ARCHIVE

Against the sun shot in Bushwick Brooklyn.

Some HDR experimentation at South Street Seaport.

Heading back to our cruise ship in Costa Maya, Mexico.

There's something peaceful about waiting at a gate.

Eating is not the only thing to do on a cruise ship.

The ambience onboard a cruise ship is unlike anything else.

When you start out blogging, it can take time to build an audience, so until you are regularly getting a good number of visitors to your blog, it may not be an attractive proposition to advertisers or ad serving networks. You have no choice but to work hard on attracting more readers. Back to traffic school: crank up the content, make sure your blog is optimized for search engines, and get socializing!

If you would rather not be at the mercy of an ad network, or if you would rather have complete control over who you wish to show ads for on your blog, then you could go down the route of selling your own ad space or sponsorship packages.

This can work really well in the blogosphere as it is also a great way of connecting with others in your creative niche. You would need to shop around to find out the going rates, decide what space you can offer, and the terms. If you don't have a big audience yet, you could start by approaching similar small blogs in your niche and see if they are interested in forming a reciprocal network or blog ring, whereby you advertise for free on each others' sites. When your visitor numbers start to build you'll be in a better position to start charging for ads, because you will have some data on how many people have clicked on the blog ring ads. It will also appear that you already have ads on the site, which could help to reassure a prospective advertiser that yours is a good site to be on.

However, as with all kinds of advertising, it is a numbers game. Put yourself in the shoes of the advertiser. It's natural to want to know how many visits your site gets a month. But if you can't demonstrate high visitor numbers, don't be disheartened. You might still have a decent click-through rate, which you could argue is just as important, if not more so, than impressions (the number of times an ad is shown).

NEED TO KNOW: COOKIES

Cookies attract a lot of bad press, but much of our browsing experience depends on them. A cookie is a small text file which websites use to "remember" you. A cookie is placed on your computer by the browser the first time you visit a site that uses them. The cookie contains the site name and a unique identifier. On subsequent visits, the browser will look to see if your computer has a cookie from that site, and if it does, it uses it to customize your experience. Cookies are used in affiliate marketing to ensure an affiliate gets paid the correct commission: if someone clicks on an ad on your site and makes a purchase, even if it's some time later and after visiting other sites, the sale should still be credited to you. There is a minefield of changing legislation around cookies, so if your site uses them ensure your privacy policy is up to date.

The Clothes Horse.
http://theclothes.blogspot.com
The Clothes Horse sets out detailed information for potential advertisers, from visitors and social media statistics to where the blog has featured, in print and online.

About: The Clothes Horse is a personal style blog updated daily that reaches more than 10,000 people every day through Google Reader and direct visits.
For specific rates e-mail me: thenewclotheshorse (at) yahoo (dot) com

Recent Statistics:
- 6,372 average daily visitors
- 435,971 average monthly actions
- 10,758 subscribers on RSS
- 5,462 followers on Blogger
- 26,104 followers on Tumblr
- 5,659 followers on Twitter
- 3,961 followers on Blog Lovin'

Advertising Options:
- two banner ad sizes available
- posts: giveaways, discount codes, integrated pieces

In Print:
BUST magazine
Elle Canada
Glamour Magazine Greece
Ellegirl Korea
Girlfriend Magazine
What I Wore Today
Sofis Mode
Vintage Affair

Online Media:
Refinery 29
Glamour Paris

EXPERT TIP: MOLLIE JOHANSON

Blog: Wild Olive
http://wildolive.blogspot.com
Started: 2004
Topic: Craft

"When monetizing your blog, I think it's important to remember that it doesn't have to be only about building income, but also building community. Through my sponsors, I've gotten to know some really great people and their blogs, and my readers have too. Sure, I've gotten some financial help that takes care of blogging expenses, but the blogging community is supportive in many ways, and it's not always about the money."

Credentials: Mollie Johanson, a trained graphic designer specializing in print projects, began her blog Wild Olive as an outlet for more whimsical works. Daily dreaming and doodling have resulted in a variety of embroidery and paper projects, most featuring simply expressive faces. Mollie, based in a far western suburb of Chicago, commutes daily to her in-home studio via the coffee pot.

GETTING PAID TO BLOG

Should you accept payment or other compensation in return for a review or endorsement of other people's products or services? This is a hot potato, much debated in the blogosphere.

Your first reaction might be at either end of the spectrum, from "No way!" to "Why not?" But wait—there's plenty of gray area in the middle. Imagine this scenario, and how you would respond: a well-known company has a new product it would like you to try out and review on your blog. You're told there is no pressure to write a good review—you can keep the product (retail price $100) either way, and you may be asked to review more things in the future, in return for a link from the company's website and free "review copies." It's a product that fits well with your blog's theme and the profile you are trying to build.

What would you say?

1. *Yes, and you would try to give it a sympathetic review even if it didn't blow you away.*
2. *Yes, and you would be brutally honest in the review, even if it might mean you wouldn't get any more review requests from that company.*
3. *You would write a positive review but only in return for a cash payment, because it would be an advertisement and you charge for advertising.*
4. *No, because you would feel an obligation to the company and you want your blogging voice to be 100% objective.*
5. *No, because ads are ads and editorial is editorial—why are your advertisers paying for it if others can sneak in adverts for free?*

Or maybe you have another response . . . there are many ways of looking at this issue.

If you want to make money from your blog and have no qualms about endorsements, there are certainly companies out there who are very interested in reaching the kind of niche communities that blogs represent. It's called "blogger outreach." As your blog becomes more visible and successful, the more likely you are to be contacted and asked to trial and review products, write guest posts on company blogs, or "sponsored" articles.

When you're a relatively new blogger, it can be flattering and exciting to be given stuff for free and asked for your opinion on it. Would you ask for payment as well? Probably not. A link from the company's website, maybe. And an enterprising blogger might make more of his or her newfound "reviewer" status with clever PR.

When you've been blogger for longer and have built up a loyal readership, you may feel differently about the value exchange. How will it look to your readers? How important is a backlink anyway? If you'd like to say yes but are worried about how your blog readers might respond, you can always write a post about the issue and ask for their comments. Or you can just do what you want—it's your blog after all, so you set the rules!

If you don't feel happy doing paid endorsements, just explain your policy. Many bloggers do this on their "about" or "sponsorship" page. That way, you are less likely to be approached.

If you do receive compensation in return for reviews, even if you have been impartial, you may be required to disclose that fact—do check what the rules are in your country. Even if it's not a legal requirement, I would still recommend telling people that you occasionally accept compensation for reviews or endorsements. That way it's out in the open and no one can say you have concealed anything. Remember, transparency and honesty are the golden rules of the social web.

Services such as that offered by http://payperpost.com, http://www.sponsoredreviews.com, and http://www.blogadvertisingstore.com put advertisers in touch with bloggers wishing to get paid to blog.

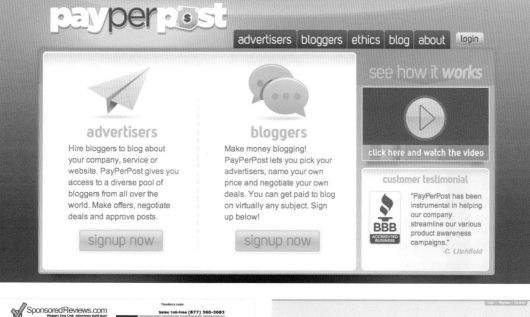

WHAT ELSE CAN YOU SELL?

The more you blog, the more you are building something of value. As a creative person, chances are you take pride in the intrinsic value of things.

But unless you are also a business person, the monetary value of your own work may not be a major consideration. When I say "your own work," I mean not just the wonderful output of your primary creative talent, but everything you are building with your blog: reputation, goodwill, influence ... what you could term your blog's brand. When you sell advertising on your blog, in a way, you are being paid for your brand.

But the bottom line is, advertisers are paying for your readers.

So what else can you sell, apart from your readers? Which, let's face it, may not be plentiful.

The obvious thing is to sell whatever it is you're creating. Many hobby bloggers get into selling, even if it wasn't their original intention. You don't have to turn your blog into an ecommerce site, but you might link it to your Etsy store. Or, if you're only selling one or two things, such as a book, you might promote it on your site but link to a bookstore for those wishing to buy. Self-publishing is a whole other area worth looking into if you want to get your recipes/photos/art/expertise out there, although you will have to do all the promotion yourself. For some, this is a route to a new career as an author, but you should also look upon it as a PR exercise as it may not make you much money.

If you do want to sell things on your blog, check your blog hosting service allows that, and, if so, what functionality is offered by the blog host or the particular theme you have in mind—there may well be a shopping cart plugin you can install, for example.

Now think about all the secondary skills you develop along the blogging journey. For example, a food blogger might become a highly accomplished photographer. A designer may discover a talent for video production. A crafter might find she's a great teacher. And just about any kind of blogger can turn into a skilled writer, editor, publicist, manager, and even psychologist!

Can any of this really be turned into cash? Certainly! Many bloggers featured in this book, who started out simply blogging about what interested them, have been paid to:

- *write books*
- *write recipes*
- *write reviews and articles in print magazines*
- *create artworks*
- *teach courses*
- *speak at conferences*
- *license their photos*

Food Wishes. http://foodwishes.blogspot.com
Chef John's Food Wishes YouTube Channel.

. . . and those are just some examples. People have found dream jobs as a result of blogging about their passion. They've also built up very attractive brands. When Chef John Mitzewich started his blog Food Wishes featuring recipe videos, little did he expect a few years later to have his blog content bought up by Allrecipes. com, the world's largest food-based social network. But it happened.

EXPERT TIP: DIANNE JACOB

Blog: Will Write for Food
http://diannej.com/blog
Started: 2009
Topic: Food

"Many bloggers resist the idea of selling their recipes, patterns, and other intellectual property; they would rather give it away for the goodwill or 'connection.' But if a company can make money from your work, why should you not be paid? It's worth asking if there is a budget. This moment can be the turning point for many bloggers, who think of themselves as hobbyists, and then find that people are willing to pay for their work. And they should. Just because writing recipes (or creating patterns/designing interiors) is your passion, it doesn't mean you should do so for free outside of your blog."

Credentials: Dianne Jacob coaches writers at all levels, whether for blogging, freelancing, or books. She has had a distinguished career in publishing and is a successful author, freelance writer, and editor. Dianne started writing about food in 1978 and since has written freelance restaurant reviews, essays, profiles, how-to pieces, recipe columns, and co-authored a cookbook, *Grilled Pizzas & Piadinas*. An experienced speaker and instructor, Dianne has taught classes and led panels at conferences and events across the US, Canada, and Mexico.

Simply Hue. http://matissecolor.blogspot.com
Vicki Dvorak sells her Creativity e-Courses via a prominent badge on her blog Simply Hue and a link on the main menu bar.

CHAPTER TEN:
PR AND YOUR BLOG

At the end of Chapter 7 I talked briefly about the importance of building offline relationships with fellow bloggers and with the media.

Good PR (free publicity, earned media . . . it goes by many names) will help to promote your blog and bring you more readers. But your blog is also a PR tool—for you, for your area of interest, for your business. An experienced and successful blogger is not only a media-owner commanding a loyal audience, but is also likely to enjoy a close relationship with journalists in their locale and industry sector. So how does this come about?

The first thing to understand is how the media landscape is changing. It has been happening for a while, and it's happening fast.

PR basics and how things are changing

In the past, PR (press relations, or public relations) was how businesses would get editorial coverage in the print media, TV, or radio. Someone responsible for PR at the organization, or an agency working on its behalf, would approach journalists with news or feature ideas. The journalists would decide whether or not to cover it, and they might put their own "spin" on it (present it in a way that would best interest their audience).

That is PR in a nutshell, but the basis of the whole process lies with the success (or otherwise) of individual relationships. There is often a natural tension between businesses and the PR practitioners looking to promote their interests, and journalists looking to serve their audience and various stakeholders. Journalists complain about pushy PR people, irrelevant press releases, and businesses expecting editorial coverage when there is

Blogger PR Wire. http://blogprwire.com
A service for bloggers who want to hear about PR pitches that they can use as content on their blogs, in the shape of features, news, giveaways, charity appeals, and more.

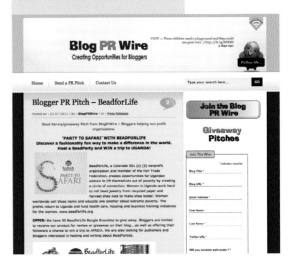

**Good, Bad and Fab.
http://www.goodbadandfab.com**
Blogger and fashion lawyer Jenny Wu makes use of PR pitches on her blog Good, Bad and Fab.

no actual news to report. Businesses and individuals looking to gain media coverage complain that their press releases are ignored or their stories twisted to the journalist's own angle.

But despite the tension, both parties needed one another. Overworked journalists depended on PR sources to supply them with a constant stream of potential material. Organizations wanting free editorial coverage knew they had to spend time cultivating friendly media contacts.

And now? Thanks to the internet, we are now all potential publishers. Your blog is your own mouthpiece and through it you can build up your own audience. If what you have to say or show is interesting, it will be shared and shared again. Those media channels that used to be so vital to get your message across, on the face of it, now become less important.

Hold it right there, though—PR is changing, but it's not dead yet! Even though bloggers are able to speak directly to people, it takes time and effort to get your blog known. Plus, the traditional media aren't going away—they still command relatively large general audiences, so you still need to be friends with them. But the difference now is that bloggers are potentially in more of a partnership with the mainstream media, as these diagrams show.

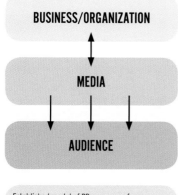

Established model of PR: messages from an organization reach the general public via the media/publisher.

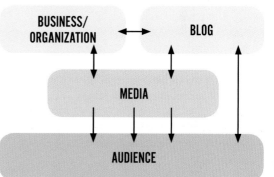

A business blog is a direct connection with the audience and has the potential for real dialogue, less easy in the one-way broadcast model of traditional media. But it doesn't replace the role of mainstream media entirely. Blogs are also potentially a rich resource for journalists.

YOUR BLOG AS A PR TOOL

Many of the bloggers featured in this book are essentially hobby or journal bloggers who have taken it further, and some started from the point of an existing business but saw the opportunity offered by having a parallel blog.

Whether deliberate or not, their blogs have become fantastic PR tools for the blogger's business, or their art, or their expertise.

Everything that happens on your blog can affect people's perceptions of your reputation and whatever it is you're selling. That's also the case elsewhere online (on social networks, for example), but the difference is that your blog is within your control—it is literally your domain.

Building a successful blog that commands the attention of the mainstream media will help you to reach new audiences and grow your reputation. Of course, the benefits of PR are hard to measure, but all kinds of things can and do happen once your blog starts attracting press coverage.

Here are just some of them, as identified by Elena Verlee of Cross Border Communications (http://www.crossborderpr.com), who blogs at PR in Your Pajamas (http://prinyourpajamas.com).

You have more clout
- *The media start to call you instead of you calling them.*
- *More prestigious magazines and larger newspapers start to cover you.*
- *Bigger TV and radio shows want to feature you.*
- *You're offered a column in a magazine or paper for your expertise.*
- *You're offered a TV or radio show.*
- *You're invited to speak at events e.g. conferences.*
- *You can charge for your speaking engagements and charge higher rates.*

PR in Your Pajamas.
http://prinyourpajamas.com
Elena Verlee's blog offers PR advice to small businesses and entrepreneurs to help them get heard and get known.

People want to work with you
- *You attract more people wanting to do joint ventures with you.*
- *You attract a higher level of partners wanting to work with you.*
- *More partners want to promote your services or carry your products.*
- *Partners and vendors offer you discounts so they can work with you.*
- *You attract investors to your company.*
- *You attract better staff wanting to work for you.*
- *Your staff is proud to represent you and stay with you longer.*

Sales become easier

- *Potential clients are "pre-sold" when they call you.*
- *Those on the fence about working with you, now buy.*
- *Clients pay for your consulting—at higher prices than before.*
- *People recommend you to their friends, family, followers, and fans.*

Making the connection

If you yearn to be featured in the style press or get nominated for an award, there are steps you can take to help your blog's chances of being spotted.

If you're a woman, join a community such as BlogHer or MomDot, where there are opportunities to make your blog standout. The first port of call for many PR companies is often a blog community. It saves time searching for blogs and quite often there's a promise (if not a guarantee) of quality.

Blog communities are keen to facilitate this, as in turn it helps to grow their profile. For example, MomDot keeps a list of "PR friendly bloggers" who welcome PR approaches. Just submit your blog and if they think it's good enough, you'll be added to the list. See http://www.momdot.com/pr-friendly-blogs.

SheBlogs (http://sheblogs.org) is another service that specifically looks to connect women bloggers with marketing and PR professionals. Similarly, BlogFriendlyPR invites influential bloggers to join their community dedicated to promoting "opportunities, sponsored placement, and exclusive campaigns to help you grow and succeed." See http://blogfriendlypr.com for more details.

SheBlogs. http://sheblogs.org
Boasting a community of more than 5000 members, SheBlogs connects female bloggers with PR and marketing professionals.

Blog Friendly PR. http://blogfriendlypr.com
Blog Friendly PR is a blog community that notifies members of PR opportunities. They offer a choice between a free or premium "Elite" service.

FOUR WAYS TO MAKE JOURNALISTS LOVE YOUR BLOG

Successful bloggers work in partnership with the mainstream media. So what can you do to make journalists love your blog?

1. Create great content worth their attention

Forget posting bland press releases on your blog. Although a well written press release can be a godsend for the stressed out hack on a tight deadline, it's never really going to be mistaken for editorial. A press release is always one-sided and often self-congratulatory, and is written in a formulaic way with conventions such as the obligatory quote.

Instead, why not offer to contribute to the publication's blog, or write a regular column on what it takes to run a blog? Or, if your industry press is more appropriate for your audience, approach magazines in your niche to see if you can work with them in some way. Offering something that will interest their readers is one way of starting a relationship with print publications and can lead to excellent publicity for your blog.

What you really want is for journalists to be curious about your work and want to tell their audience about it. If the quality of content and presentation on your blog is excellent and unique, it will immediately standout from the majority of blogs.

2. Make your blog posts jump out in searches

Think about what journalists are likely to be looking for, and the search terms they might use. If it's news coverage you're after, write about newsworthy topics that tie in to local or national news. If you're courting industry or trade press, blog about the hot topics, what people are talking about, what you learned at a recent conference, or emerging trends. Most importantly, think about your key words or phrases and put them in the blog post heading and body copy: just one or two key phrases per post, no more.

3. Know where the journalists hangout

One way of developing a useful relationship with individuals in the media is to think about where they spend their time online, what communities they are members of, who else is in their network, and who influences them. It's easier than it sounds, now that social channels such as Twitter have become mainstream tools for journalists. Following someone on Twitter, seeing their conversations, being ready to respond if they ask a question, perusing their lists of contacts . . . this can help build up a picture of the individual, from what they are working on at the moment to which conferences they attend. If you get the opportunity to introduce yourself at an event, do so. You may be surprised—they may already be aware of you.

4. Make life easy for them

So, a researcher for The Martha Stewart Show arrives at your blog and loves what she finds there. Now what? Journalists and researchers are always short of time. Don't make it hard for them to contact you or find what they need. As your blog grows in popularity you will need to make some compromises: email addresses can be harvested and spammed, but if a contact email is both hard to find and non-clickable (as in "email me at info (at) myblog (dot) com") then that might be the point at which the media person clicks away to another blog and you've lost the opportunity. Some bloggers have a "press" page with links to downloadable long and short bios and a library of low resolution versions of images for the media to use. It means they can quickly choose one or two images and request high resolution versions.

Another way you can become indispensible to the media is to respect their publishing schedules and anticipate their needs ahead of time. Print magazines often have forward features lists, which are really to help sell advertising, but if you can get hold of them they will tell you what topics are coming up. If you have an idea for an on-topic feature or article that will be of interest to their audience, suggest it.

Listorious. http://listorious.com
At Listorious you can search for Twitter lists of journalists, such as this list of 500 UK journalists created by Sue Llewellyn.

CHAPTER ELEVEN:
MONITORING YOUR BLOG'S PERFORMANCE

Metrics, analytics, sheesh! Do you really need to worry about all that? Possibly not, but stay with me for a while, you might be surprised!

It's human nature to make comparisons. I defy any blogger to say that they never look at another blog and think their own might be lacking in some way. An essential part of blogging is making connections and learning from others, and it doesn't have to be a rivalry. For some of us, always trying to go a few steps further or overcome the next challenge, whether competing against ourselves or others, is an enjoyable part of the game. A little bit of measuring up goes a long way.

There's an old story which goes something like this: a driver on a country road stops a man walking his dog to ask the way. "How do I get to Newtown?" he says, and the man answers, "If I were you I wouldn't start from here!" Helpful, huh? When you start on your blog, you're on a journey to somewhere. And knowing if you're on the right track and how much further you have to go can be very reassuring, particularly on those days when you have a hundred other priorities, or when something about the blog is getting you down.

If you are blogging for business, the idea of having measurable objectives won't be new. But if you're blogging to follow your passion, to share something you love with the world, is it worth measuring anything?

I think the answer is yes, but you need to decide WHAT to measure. Even if you don't have a specific goal to aim for, such as "to generate $X worth of business from my blog," you can still have ideas about where you want your blog to take you.

The stats themselves can actually be a bit addictive and you can end up wasting a lot of time, so it's best to identify early on what stats are important to monitor, and which you can ignore. If words like "metrics" and "benchmarking" make your eyes glaze over, not to worry: opposite is a short diagnostic questionnaire to help you get going. Jot down your answers. (Don't spend too long thinking about it, and keep them brief.)

You should see a pattern emerging—these three questions are all aspects of the same thing, which is what you want your blog to achieve, or your key goal or goals. The next step is to ask the question: how will I know if I am on the path to achieving this goal?

The main reason I want a blog is:

....

....

....

....

(**For example:** *to share my work with the world, to get feedback on work-in-progress, to build a reputation as an expert, to get me a book deal, to build a community of like-minded people, to drive sales on my website . . .)*

My blog will be beneficial to me / my business because it will:

....

....

....

....

(**For example:** *show a wide range of my work to a larger audience, be discovered and read by journalists who will write about me/my work/my business, make me money . . .)*

In three years' time, my blog will:

....

....

....

....

(**For example:** *be essential reading for thousands of people, be in the "top ten blogs" for my industry, be a significant income stream, have a team of regular contributors, be a big, beautiful archive of my work . . .)*

WHAT SHOULD YOU MEASURE?

I'm going to take three examples of goals and show you how you might work out the most important things to measure.

Example Goal #1:
to share my work with the world
How I will know if I'm on my way:
- *Visibility in searches is improving*
- *Visitors numbers are always increasing*
- *Visitors come from all over the world*
- *Subscriber numbers are increasing*
- *Email newsletter signups are increasing*
- *Blog posts are being shared on other blogs and social networks*

What I need to measure:
- *Blog visibility (search rankings)*
- *Visitor numbers*
- *Countries where visitors are coming from*
- *Subscriber numbers*
- *Email sign ups*
- *Numbers of retweets, reblogs, shared links, mentions on social networks*
- *Number of comments*

Example Goal #2:
to be one of the top 10 blogs in my niche
How I will know if I'm on my way:
- *My blog is getting the attention of influencers in my niche*
- *Other blogs are referencing my blog as an authority*
- *My blog posts are being shared on other blogs and social networks*

SAY 100. http://say100.saymedia.com
Something to aspire to? The SAY 100 is a list of "knowledgeable online voices that create engaging content, drive conversation, and shape opinion."

- *I am being approached by potential advertisers and guest contributors*
- *The number and quality of comments is increasing*

What I need to measure:
- *Number of mentions by named influencers (need to identify who they are)*
- *Quality of blogs and sites where blog is being referenced and of sites giving trackbacks*
- *Frequency of approaches received by people interested in working with/for the blog*
- *Number and quality of comments*

Example Goal #3:
to be a significant income stream
How I will know if I'm on my way:
- *Blog visibility in searches constantly improving*
- *Visitor numbers increasing significantly*
- *Income from advertising is increasing*
- *Sales from blog visitors increasing*
- *Requests for paid reviews or paid links increasing*

What I need to measure:
- *Blog visibility (search rankings)*
- *Visitor numbers*
- *Ad revenue*
- *Quantity of traffic being passed from blog to site where sales take place*
- *Sales resulting from blog referrals*
- *Number/frequency of paid opportunities offered*

The types of data available can be grouped into visibility (search rankings and inbound links), traffic (visits), engagement (time on page, comments, shares, referrals), and conversion (subscribers, sales).

Get the picture? Now you have an idea of what you can and should be measuring, let's go ahead and look at how to do it.

EXPERT TIP: MICHELLE MINNAAR

Blog: Greedy Gourmet
http://www.greedygourmet.com
Started: 2007
Topic: Food

"Most blogs use Google Analytics to measure traffic. Other bloggers track the growth of their RSS and newsletter readership, or boast about the number of Twitter followers or Facebook fans they have. There has been a sad case where a blogger stopped blogging because she felt not enough people commented on her site. What is actually the most important factor regarding your blog's success is how you feel about it. If you find something lacking, improve that component. Otherwise if you're happy with your blog, it's successful! What more do you have to prove?"

Credentials: Michelle Minnaar is a professional photographer who loves to cook. When she's not looking after her two children, she blogs and reviews restaurants. As one of the most popular food blogs in the UK, Greedy Gourmet publishes family-friendly recipes, great giveaways, insightful reviews, and a weekly newsletter.

TOOLS FOR THE JOB

Blog hosting provider: basic traffic & engagement

Blog hosts provide basic information about who is visiting your blog (or what, in the case of indexing crawlers or "bots"). It's often referred to as "traffic," although personally I prefer to think of it in more human terms!

Analytics services, free and paid:
traffic & engagement, conversion

You may find you want to know more than your blog host stats can tell you, in which case you might decide to install analytics software on your blog. The most commonly used analytics tool is Google Analytics (http://google.com/analytics), which is free. More about this in a moment.

If you would rather not rely on Google Analytics but are keen to monitor detailed statistics, such as how

Blogger
Blogger has a Stats function where you can view traffic sources and page views.

WordPress.com
WordPress.com has a Stats feature built in, or you can install it as a plugin on a self-hosted WordPress blog.

Typepad
In Typepad's Overview you see a snapshot of your blog's traffic and shares, with the option to download the detail of the data.

long people stay on a particular blog post or how far down the page they scroll, take a look at paid tools such as Chartbeat (http://chartbeat.com).

To keep an eye on how many people are subscribing to your blog, Feedburner (http://feedburner.google.com) is a useful free tool. You will need the address of your RSS feed—when you submit that to Feedburner it gives you a new Feedburner RSS feed address, which is what you should then use on your blog wherever you have the "subscribe" button.

Links & SEO analytics services: visibility

Measuring your blog's performance in search engines can be done manually, and for many bloggers this is sufficient. But much of the work can be automated and consequently there are many free tools to help you with optimizing your blog for search engines, and diagnosing any issues. Check out SEO Book (http://tools.seobook.com). It's a subscription service for website owners wanting to do their own SEO, but it also offers a range of free web-based tools, from one that shows how your blog appears to search engine spiders to a "meta tag generator" tool.

If you are looking to make money from your blog, then being found in searches will be more crucial and you might find it a great help to use one of the paid tools available. LinkDex (http://www.linkdex.com), for example, helps with all aspects of search engine optimization for your blog, including things are are not usually included in the free tools, such as analyzing inbound links to your blog and other blogs, and how this compares to "competitors."

Chartbeat
Chartbeat is an analytics tool used by a number of pro bloggers.

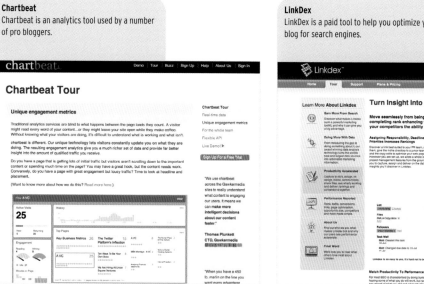

LinkDex
LinkDex is a paid tool to help you optimize your blog for search engines.

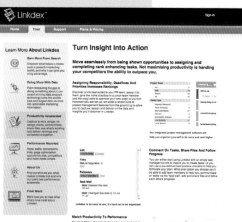

SETTING UP GOOGLE ANALYTICS

Google Analytics is a free, web-based tool with which you can find out a huge amount of information about who is visiting your blog; where they are coming from, the keywords they use, which pages they view, and much more.

A note if you're using WordPress: although WordPress.com does not allow Google Analytics, it does have its own stats package which you can access from your Dashboard. Alternatively, if you use WordPress blogware from WordPress.org, self hosted on your own domain, you can install the Google Analytics plugin.

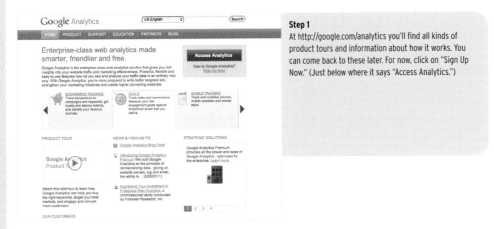

Step 1
At http://google.com/analytics you'll find all kinds of product tours and information about how it works. You can come back to these later. For now, click on "Sign Up Now." (Just below where it says "Access Analytics.")

Step 2
On the next screen, you will be told that you need a Google account in order to sign up for Google Analytics. If you have one, click on "sign in here," otherwise you need to fill this page out to create your Google account. This is not the same as your Google Analytics account, but having a Google account gets you access to all kinds of services. (See p. 41, Take it Further.)

Step 3

Next you will see a screen like this, inviting you to sign up for Google Analytics itself. Just hit the "Sign up" button and you're nearly there . . .

Step 4

You're now on the Google Analytics "Create Account" screen. Give your account a name, and enter the URL of your blog, your country, and time zone.

Under "Data Sharing Settings" you have the choice of keeping your data entirely private, or shared across other Google services, or as anonymous data that Google aggregates as part of the way it monitors industry trends.

Then select your country for the user agreement, read the Terms and Conditions, and, if you agree, check the box and hit "Create Account."

Step 5

Congratulations! You are now into Google Analytics. You should see your blog name and address at the top right of the page. Before you start exploring, you need to get the tracking code that goes on your blog.

Step 6

It's a good idea to copy the code snippet under "Paste this code into your site" and save it in a plain text file (Notepad or Text Edit).

Installing the tracking code on your blog

Take a look at the code snippet you've just copied—it contains your unique identifier or ID, which looks something like this (with numbers instead of Xs):

UA - XXXXXXXX - X

Alternatively, Google Analytics includes a handy email, already written, for you to send these instructions— just click on "email these instructions" and send them to yourself. If you have someone technical helping you out who will know how to install Google Analytics, send them the email as well.

The next step is to place the code snippet in the correct place on your blog. This will vary depending on your blog host or theme. Below and opposite, shows you how to install Google Analytics on Typepad, Blogger, or Tumblr.

Once you have installed Google Analytics on your blog, wait 24 hours, then check back into Google Analytics to make sure the tracking code is working. When you log in, go to "Dashboard" and you should see the name of your blog top right. Click on the "cog" icon next to it, and on the next page select "Tracking."

Typepad
Installing Google Analytics on a Typepad blog is very easy. Go to your blog "Settings" and select "Add Ons," then simply enter your ID number and save.

TypePad® Dashboard Blogs ▼ Library ▼   Robin Houghton Account Help Sign Out

Regency Costume   Compose ▼   Overview Posts Comments Design Settings   View blog ➡

Basics
SEO
Sharing
Feeds
Add-Ons ○
Posts
Categories
Comments
Authors
Post by Email
Import/Export

Add-Ons

Google Analytics

Use Google Analytics in addition to stats on TypePad for a comprehensive view of the visitors to your blog. Learn more about Google Analytics.

UA Number: [   ]

Note: For Pro plans, if you have previously added the Google Analytics tracking code via TypeLists or Advanced Templates, you should remove it if you plan on adding the same code here.

Typekit Fonts

Using Typekit, you can add custom fonts to your blog design. Learn more about Typekit.

Typekit Kit ID: [   ]

Note: Enter the Typekit Kit ID which corresponds to this blog domain and the embed code will be added to your blog.

(Save Changes)

Help with Add-Ons

What is Google Analytics?
Google Analytics is a third-party web analytics solution that provides website traffic reporting. Get Started.

Note: If you are creating a Google Analytics account for the first time, do not follow the "Add Tracking" steps. Select "Finish" to retrieve your UA number.

How to find your UA number
UA numbers are listed in the "Accounts" table under "Name". If you see a display name or the URL to your blog instead, then you will need to click into the specific account to view the UA number.

What is Typekit?
Typekit is the easiest way to use real fonts on your website. With a Typekit subscription, you can use custom fonts in your blog design. Learn more.

Blogger: Step 1

You will need to have your Google Analytics code snippet at the ready. Log in and select "Template" from your main menu.

Click on "Edit HTML"–you will get a warning about messing about with the code, just ignore that. The source code of the template is then revealed to you.

Blogger: Step 2

Now do this next bit very carefully. Scroll down until you see the closing </head> tag. It may be a long way down. Then put your cursor there and paste in the Google Analytics code snippet. It starts with <script type="text/javascript"> and ends with </script>. Save your template, and you're done.

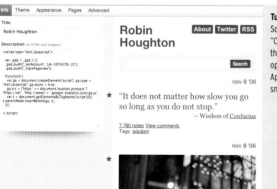

Tumblr

Some Tumblr themes have an option under "Appearance"–"Customize" for you to add your Google Analytics ID. If the theme you are using does not, simply click on the Preferences option on the Dashboard (a cog), and then "Customize Appearance" –"Info." Paste your Google Analytics code snippet into the "Description" field and save changes.

CHAPTER TWELVE:
TROUBLESHOOTING

"There may be trouble ahead . . . " No matter how enthusiastic you are about your blog, and passionate about your interests, every now and again you'll have to figure something out and it won't always be easy!

When you're starting out, the primary issues are likely to be to do with getting familiar with the technology, experimenting with content, and organizing your time. I hope this book will be a resource that you can dip into for inspiration and explanation, and of course you will continue to update your learning. Technology, in particular, changes at such a pace that even during the writing of this book I've had to go back and revise the advice in places, or retake screenshots.

You also need to be aware of the legal aspects of blogging, which include things like copyright and attribution, disclosure, and privacy. I'm not saying you have to get specialist training or employ a lawyer, but you do need to familiarize yourself with the basics of what you can and can't do within the law. I can tell you what you need to be aware of, but you should always check your local laws because they can be different from country to country, state to state.

As you settle into a blogging routine, learning what works for you and your readers, connecting with other bloggers, you will become more practiced and confident. Tech issues may be less daunting, or if you need help you'll know where to go for it.

However, as your blog becomes more successful so will your exposure, which can have its share of downsides. It's a sad fact that online, human nature is exposed not only in all its glory but also in all its ugliness.

But it's not all bad—for the majority of bloggers, the joy of blogging and the wonderful connections it brings far outweigh the negatives.

In this chapter I will highlight the key issues that bloggers can come up against and suggest how to pre-empt or prepare for potential problems. We'll also look at how successful bloggers have dealt with difficult situations and what has worked for them.

EXPERT TIP: TARA HOGAN

Blog: INK+WIT
http://inkandwit.blogspot.com
Started: 2004
Topic: Design & Stationery

"When I first started blogging I posted and wrote about a few websites and products purely to help promote those who wrote in to INK+WIT. I didn't want to hurt anyone's feelings. Instead of writing the person back and saying, 'I do not feel it fits the blog aesthetic or content,' I thought it would be nice to help them out. After a few months I realized that although it is hard to say no you cannot please everyone and it is important to maintain the integrity of your own premise, business, and goals. If you go against the foundation of what you are making, it will fall apart and quality will go down. It is wise to give everyone a fair chance, but be honest about why you may not post them. This is constructive criticism."

Credentials: INK+WIT is a boutique design space founded by designer and illustrator, Tara Hogan. Her blog focuses on that which is sustainable, valuable, essential, and inspiring on the material and ethereal plain. The blog accompanies Tara's eponymous design business.

RESPECTING THE LAW

I have touched on legal issues at various times throughout this book. First of all, my own disclaimer: I am not offering legal advice or counsel of any kind, but if there is one piece of advice you take from me here it should be to check what the law requires where you are—it may be different from that of another country. Just because the internet crosses borders, the laws governing websites (including blogs) do not.

So what are the most common issues newbie bloggers come up against?

Copyright

This is a big one. Copyright covers all kinds of intellectual property (IP)—the definition of which is disputable, but generally speaking, refers to anything that someone has created from scratch, including articles, music, recordings, video, logos, trademarks, and more.

Be aware that if you are blogging from a mobile device and using a third-party application such as TwitPic or Instagram, you may be waiving some of your rights, so do read the Terms and Conditions. Also, if you upload content by mobile phone you are inviting people to share it, but people won't always think to attribute the work to you.

If you are a victim of copyright infringement, you have the option to take action, but what kind would probably depend on who did it and what form it took. In the case of one blogger to another, it might be enough to make a simple request to either remove the item or acknowledge the work as yours. But if you feel exploited and that someone is profiting from your work, it's worth seeking legal advice.

On the other hand, it cuts both ways. As I mentioned in Chapter 5, just because it's easy to go lifting stuff from around the web, that doesn't make it legal. Many small-scale bloggers and site owners use Google Image

Compfight. http://compfight.com
Compfight is a useful image search engine that allows you to tailor your search to images licenced under Creative Commons. A search for "cake decoration" produces just under 2,000 images.

search to find images, copy them, and use them with abandon, without any kind of attribution.

Make no mistake, this is not good practice. I've heard of enough cases where copyright infringement has been pursued, usually (in the case of a small-time blogger) only as far as the "cease and desist" letter, but it can still be a nasty shock. Even if the original creator is long dead or unknown, chances are that someone still owns the copyright.

If you're not creating your own photos, low-cost image sources include one of the many sites offering free or cheap stock images, or Flickr. You can't just use any image on Flickr, only those that are offered under a Creative Commons licence, which means that some rights are reserved. For example. you may be able to use an image for free, in return for attribution. See http://www.flickr.com/creativecommons/ for more details about this.

Google Image Search
A Google Image search for "cake decoration" brings up nearly 4 million images, but many of them will be copyright-protected, so not free to use.

Defamation

When you settle into your blog, you may find the relaxed nature of it can lead you to let down your guard. Beware! Defamation is when you say something about someone that can harm their reputation. If you upset someone and it can be proved in court that what you said is wrong, you could be in hot water. If, however, it is simply your opinion (and you're clear about that), then you might get away with it. This is the kind of issue that publishers face every day, and as a blogger you must remember you too are a publisher. If you have guest bloggers or if you blog with other people, make sure everyone understands their responsibilities.

Privacy & disclosure

The internet is a hotbed of covert activity. Put simply, data is money. Every time we sign up for a free trial of software, hit a "Like" button on an article, click on a link, or even just search the web, our every move is recorded and turned into data that's traded between advertisers, governments, organizations, and any number of third party intermediaries.

Unsurprisingly, there is concern on all this tracking and monitoring, and privacy is a contentious issue.

If you collect data about visitors on your blog, such as through an email newsletter sign-up, you may need a statement on your blog saying how that information is used. If your blog carries affiliate ads and links, or if you receive compensation for anything you post on your blog, you will need to declare that. Rules about disclosure do vary from country to country.

Be careful when photographing or recording audio or video of people and their work, with a view to sharing it on your blog—you should ask their permission first.

Federal Trade Commission legislation in the US means that bloggers must disclose any payments they receive. Many bloggers like to handle this requirement in their own style, and with humor, such as this from http://www.deepglamour.net.

There are plenty of legal websites where you can buy an "out of the box" Privacy Policy statement for your blog for a nominal amount, such as this from http://www.legalcentre.co.uk. If you do this, be sure that the policy you are buying is suitable for use in your country.

HANDLING DIFFICULT SITUATIONS

The majority of people are considerate and grateful to bloggers for sharing their expertise, wit, art, and creativity. However, you will occasionally encounter a difficult situation. It can usually be handled quietly and swiftly, but the secret is to not take it personally or let it get you down.

Saying no

Every now and then you will get asked for something that you'd rather not give, for whatever reason. For example, someone might offer to write a guest blog post for you, or invite you to do so for them, but you don't think their blog is a good "fit" with yours—to say yes might not be good for your reputation, to say no might cause offence. This is the situation described by Tara Hogan at the start of this chapter.

Alternatively, someone you know might ask you for a link to their site, or to advertise something they are doing for charity, or to "like" something of theirs. Again, the risk to you is that you dilute the quality of your blog, or not be true to what you really think. A Facebook "Like" or a Google +1 is, after all, not just saying you like something, but a public endorsement and recommendation to your friends.

You may get approached by companies or PR people wanting you to write a paid review, or cover an event on their behalf.

What to do: As long as you are clear in your mind what you consider as being true to you, your blog, and your readers, you should feel comfortable saying either yes or no. You may wish to, but don't feel you have to explain or defend your decision.

It's a good idea to pre-empt these kinds of situations by spelling out your policy on your blog, rather like one of those signs you might see at the convenience store saying, "Please do not ask for credit as refusal often offends."

Flaming & trolling

Your blog is your own voice, and it's likely that not everyone will agree with everything you say all of the time. Dealing with rude or critical comments can be one of the hardest things about blogging, especially if it seems to be personal.

This kind of thing (also known as "flaming") has been around since the start of the internet, when people could hide behind anonymous avatars and made-up names. Sometimes arguments even break out between commenters, which then tends to attract other forms of antisocial behavior, such as writing something contentious just to get a reaction, or hijacking the discussion (also known as "trolling".)

What to do: Look at your comments settings—most blog software allows you to moderate comments before they go live. You can also ensure that people have to enter an email address before they can post, or sign in with other ID, such as Twitter or Facebook.

If someone leaves a negative comment, you might still decide to publish it if it's legitimate criticism, so that you can address it. Even if it's unreasonable, it can still be worth publishing as it shows that you're open and willing to face your critics. Answer the criticism publicly and politely and close the comments. Dealing with difficult people in front of an audience can undermine them and earn you a huge amount of respect from sympathetic onlookers.

Controversial subject matter can bring out strong comments, which bloggers usually elect to deal with on the blog, or let other commenters deal with, rather than deleting comments (unless they are libelous).

12-20-2006 @2:06PM
Jessica said...
★★★ ☐ ☐ ⚐

"Almost everyone had some prior knowledge of the controversy that surrounds the delicacy, but any pangs of conscience were overridden by hunger pangs and curiosity."

Oh man, what terribly enlightened thinkers you all were to override your moral principles for a snack! Too bad you didn't have anyone on the fence at your party - you could have force fed it to them and then everyone could have understood even better how their dinner got to their plate.

Reply

12-20-2006 @2:44PM
Candace said...
★★★ ☐ ☐ ⚐

Oh Jessica give it a break. Not everyone in the world cares about the same things you do. It doesn't make you morally superior to the entire planet, though you like to think it does.

Reply

12-20-2006 @3:53PM
Jonny said...
★★★ ☐ ☐ ⚐

Come on Jessica, is how this is produced any worse than farm chickens or farm cattle? Candace, you got it right. Views like this are arrogant and misplaced.

Reply

12-20-2006 @3:40PM
Roger Thomas said...
★★★ ☐ ☐ ⚐

U make me sick! nasty! ewwww. you are horrible for eating poor ducks' most liquor processing organ. how will i get them drunk for my annual beer duck roast. Shame on UUUUU!

Reply

12-20-2006 @3:54PM
Dmnkly said...
★★★ ☐ ☐ ⚐

Nice, Jessica!

Way to show people the merit of your position through intelligent, reasoned discussion and a willingness to engage an opposing view, rather than simply asserting the truth by resorting to righteousness and hyperbole!

Oh... wait...

Reply

12-20-2006 @3:54PM
And0 said...
★★★ ☐ ☐ ⚐

Jessica, you seem to have accidentally left out the next line from your quote:
"That may be a bit of an overstatement, so let's just say that no strong feelings either way were expressed."

Doesn't sound like any moral principals were overridden.

EXPERT TIP: "MISS" JAMES KICINSKI

Blog: Bleubird Vintage
http://bleubirdvintage.typepad.com
Started: 2008
Topic: Vintage

"Having a public blog and sharing our lives for the world to see can bring judgement as well as praise. Many people who read my blog think that they know me, when in fact they only see a very small part of our story. Sometimes the opinions and criticism from commenters can be harsh, but I have to just ignore it and keep on truckin'. Not everyone is going to be supportive of our lifestyle and I'm okay with that."

Credentials: Designer and vintage collector "Miss" James Kicinski describes herself as "a seventies child living in Texas." She has been selling online from her shop Bleubird Vintage since 2005, and now focuses more on her blog which has built a large and loyal following. "Miss" James blogs about vintage style, favorite finds, and her children's lunch boxes, among over things!

STAYING MOTIVATED

It hits us all at some point—the blogging blahs. It could be caused by other things in your life taking precedence. Family upheavals and life changes, certainly. Or it might be something temporary that has disrupted your blogging routine—sickness, a computer crash, or even bad weather can leave you feeling out of sorts and not in the mood to tend your blog.

The result can be that you feel you don't have enough time to blog, that it's not a priority. But the "not enough time" excuse might not be the real reason. The real reason is just that you're uninspired.

It's a question I've asked of many bloggers. Much of the advice in this book is aimed at giving you the tools to deal with this—the planning, the content ideas, the expert tips. But is there anything else you can do to pull through and get your passion back?

Short, sharp shock

Just do it! Give yourself half an hour and get something up, even if it's bemoaning the fact that you're a bit out of love with blogging. Remind yourself that a blog post doesn't have to be perfect, but it does need to be up. Short and quick is fine—you can always fill it out later. And who knows, you may get a comment or two that will get you back in the blogging saddle.

Start another blog!

If you have a smartphone, look for a fun social app like Instagram which involves nothing more complex than taking a photo, choosing a style, and uploading it. OK, so it's another form of blogging, which sounds counter-intuitive, but it can help to restore the joy of sharing stuff, which is what you need.

Get away from it all

Go for a walk, or out with friends, and talk about something completely different. Give yourself permission not to blog, on the condition that tomorrow you sit down for half an hour and revisit the list of blog post types in Chapter 5 and choose one.

Get out your plan

Open your content plan and review. If you're way behind with it, just start again. Look for any blog post ideas from the past that you haven't acted on and bring them into your new schedule. Not got a content plan? Oh no! I hope you're reading this BEFORE you hit the bloggers' wall, because then you've got a good reason to set one up!

Think of your readers

What are they doing right now? What are they interested in? How can you help them? You've been a bit preoccupied lately, so spend a few minutes thinking of your audience and what they would like from you. Go back in time on your blog and look again at stuff you posted in the past that brought enjoyment to people, and to you. Congratulate yourself. Now do more of the same.

If all else fails . . .

- *You can always reposition and revamp previously blogged material, if you're stuck*
- *Visit some of your favorite blogs—even if it doesn't immediately inspire you, do try and leave the odd comment, as it shows you're still around in the blogosphere*
- *Re-read this book from the beginning!*

10 COMMON BLOG MISTAKES TO AVOID

The more you blog, the better you get at it. There's no right way—everyone's style is different, that's the fun of blogs. But there are some common mistakes that it's worth knowing about. You have been warned!

1) Too many gadgets and embellishments

It's so easy to add embellishments, gizmos, widgets, and other bits and bobs to your blog, and the choice is enormous. It's rather like adding apps to your phone, except that apps don't stop you from using the phone as, well, a phone. Scale it back!

2) Light text on a dark background

I've mentioned this already but it's worth saying again. Dark backgrounds are headache-inducing, not to mention tricky for the sight-impaired. Use caution.

3) Too much information

Although I always advocate a personal approach (see the next point), just beware of over-sharing. People may well be visiting your blog to be uplifted and inspired, or to escape into your world. They may not wish to hear about your family arguments, or the fact that you're feeling under the weather.

4) Not enough information

Your blog readers will be curious about you—at the very least, about who you are and how you got into blogging. If you are confident enough to reveal a little about yourself it's a sure fire way to build trust and encourage readers to comment, share, and make contact. Anyone trying to stay anonymous on the social web looks suspicious.

5) Uninspiring blog post titles

As I mentioned in Chapter 5, your blog post titles or headlines are crucial. Every word counts—in an RSS reader or in the sidebar of your blog, the title might be the only thing visible, so it has to be interesting enough to persuade someone to click and donate their valuable time to reading your blog post. Be descriptive rather than cute. Everyone hates being "tricked" into clicking.

6) Links not saying where they go

When linking to another blog or site, say where it is you're sending people. It's not sufficient to tell readers to "find out more about the exhibition here." It would be far better to say "find out more about the exhibition at the Royal Academy website" or even "find out more about the Royal Academy's Summer Show."

7) Mixing too many topics / lack of focus

There is a school of thought that says a blog should be focused on one thing, and that you should not go "off topic." But then again, I've come across many wonderful bloggers who do slip in odd details about other things they are up to, or family news, and readers love it. Just try not to blog about everything—people are more likely to come back again and again if they know pretty much what your blog is about, and that's what interests them.

8) Using automatically loading music and video

Background music, video, or animation that starts automatically can be annoying and distracting, and many people browse blogs while they are at work. So be considerate.

9) Not posting frequently enough

Yup, I'm back on this one again. It's a mistake I've made enough times—I'm putting my hand up to it! I also know that when you start posting more regularly, subscriptions, page views, and comments all tend to improve. Do whatever it takes to publish something at least once a week.

10) Spelling and grammatical errors

It just doesn't look great, does it? Ironically, I recently read a blog post on this very topic—common blogging mistakes to avoid—and there in the sidebar was the heading "Sponsers." Spelling mistakes immediately undermine a blog's credibility and could make the difference between you being offered that book deal . . . and not.

CHAPTER THIRTEEN: LET'S BLOG!

New, vibrant blogs are being launched every day, and blogging just isn't going away. As a blogger you are a citizen-publisher, outside the mainstream and perhaps under the radar of the traditional press, but a force to be reckoned with nonetheless.

Bloggers are people who care about something, and it's been said that the blogosphere is where some of the most open, challenging, and vibrant discussion about any subject takes place, not to mention some of the most innovative creative endeavors.

So, you've got the passion, you've got the tools—all you need to do is to get started. I'm sure you've heard the saying (usually attributed to Woody Allen) that "80% of success is showing up." Still feel there's something stopping you? You're not alone!

Three tips to beat procrastination

1: *Take small steps. Don't set yourself too big a task, especially at first. For example, one step might be to visit Tumblr.com, look at some Tumblr blogs, and maybe sign up so that you can have a poke around with the software. Another step might be to brainstorm blog titles with a friend, or go through a "what shall I blog about" exercise.*
2: *Find the best time. You chould be realistic about your schedule—is there a time each day when you can set aside an hour to work on your blog, without distractions? If not, then how about half an hour? Although some tasks will need longer, it's better to do half an hour a day than for weeks to go by with nothing happening on your blog. You'll also*
get familiar with blogging tools and create blogging connections more quickly.
3: *Find a blogging buddy. Make promises to each other, such as posting something each week or commenting on blogs found by one another, or find time for the occasional "cake date" when you meet and help each other out with something or explore answers to nagging "how-to" questions.*

In this book I've introduced many topics, and I'm sure there were moments when you were thinking, "Yes, but . . . I want to know more about this." I don't presume to have all the answers, and in the course of researching and writing this book I've been struck by how much I'm still learning.

But what I can do is point you toward resources that will teach you more, help you sift through the internet to find the useful stuff (much of which I've yet to find myself), and show you a few last examples of the intriguing things that bloggers get up to. All of which I hope will boost you on your blogging journey.

SHOP GIRL DIARIES
IT ALL BEGAN IN A CHANDELIER SHOP

Home News

TUESDAY, 27 SEPTEMBER 2011

My Blog Mojo

Yeah I got your
Blog Mojo - Come
and get it if you
think you're hard
enough!

I've always said, rather smugly, that I don't believe in 'Writer's Block'.

You can always write, just sometimes it's total rubbish.

Real 'Writer's Block' requires a boxer in between you and your laptop.

Yet lately I've been squirming as the time lapse between my blog posts grows.

Have I lost my blog mojo?

SUBSCRIBE TO

☐ Posts
☐ Comments

WINNER Completely Novel AUTHOR BLOG AWARDS

SHOP GIRL DIARIES ON AMAZON

If you like the blog, you'll love the book! Get your copy from Amazon.co.uk

SUBSCRIBE TO SHOP GIRL DIARIES

☐ Posts
☐ Comments

Design Mom.
http://www.designmom.com

Gabrielle Blair's blog has won numerous awards and been featured in the press and on TV. Started in 2006, when Gabrielle was thirty-one and already a mother of five, the blog continues to delight and inspire. Gabrielle has since had another baby but still manages to blog just about every day.

HOME ABOUT FAQS PRESS PICTURE BOOKS GUEST MOMS ASK DESIGN MOM   SUBSCRIBE

 DESIGN MOM

WELCOME

My name is Gabrielle Blair. I'm a designer and mother of six (our new addition was born last May). We are spending a year abroad in France. I post on where design and motherhood intersect.

Like what you see? Fantastic. Subscribe to my RSS Feed. Like me on Facebook. Follow me on Twitter. See my photos on Flickr.

SPONSORS

I'm A Giant
OCTOBER 12, 2011

Emily Henderson has the best ideas. Because she knows that the only thing more fun than decorating a home is decorating a miniature one.

Known best for her season five Design Star win and her inspiring HGTV show called Secrets From A Stylist, Emily recently came up with a brand new kind of blog challenge called I'm A Giant. She and a few other bloggers — at least four of whom you can catch at Alt Design Summit 2012 — are each designing their own dollhouses and then decorating them to the max.

Emily says it best when she explains why she'd like everyone to join in the I'm A Giant project: "It's something that we can all do together, talk about, swap stories, compete for furniture on eBay, and not feel ridiculous . . . together."

Kind of like blogging, don't you think?

Did you grow up playing with a dollhouse? Will you join in the miniature fun? Everyone's welcome. I have to admit that well-designed dollhouses make me happy, a tiny tea set, miniature clocks, and small spoons used to elicit the most girlie squeals from me!

Helpful Steps for Parents.
Learn more
BMO Harris Bank

LOOKING FOR SOMETHING?

To search, type and hit enter

HOUSE HUNTERS INTERNATIONAL

Here's something fun. Our family was featured in an episode of House Hunters International? Spoiler: we choose the gorgeous French Farmhouse. It's called La Cressonnière and we take pictures of it all the time. If you're curious, try these links:

The Kitchen
Summer at La Cressonnière
The Hallbath
The Stairwell
The Neighbors
Ralph's Bedroom

EXPERT TIP: **EMILY BENET**

Blog: Shop Girl Diaries
http://emilybenet.blogspot.com
Started: 2008
Topic: Diary

"People so often forget to establish their overall theme before launching a blog. Before starting, ask yourself: What do I know? Does it excite me? Can I sustain it (for months, years)? Once you have your big idea, think up six possible posts. If you can't think of three, then your idea might need some refining!"

Credentials: Emily Benet's book *Shop Girl Diaries* was published in 2009. The book began in June 2008 as a weekly blog about working in her mother's chandelier shop. She was approached a few months later to write a screenplay for a TV pilot, and in 2009 Salt Publishing suggested that she turn the blog into a book. Emily, a fluent Spanish speaker, is currently working on a new novel set in London and Cartagena (Colombia).

MORE BLOG INSPIRATION

Throughout this book you have been offered advice, ideas, and stories from bloggers who love what they do. Here are just a few more to inspire you: six bloggers coming at their work from different angles and with different goals, in their own words.

KEIKO OIKAWA

Blog: Nordljus
http://www.nordljus.co.uk

"I try and stick to the core concept of my blog, which is to take time and care to relate my experiences with the best of my pictures. In this sense my blog hasn't changed too much from when I started; but I think this engages my readers more than if I compromised just for the sake of posting more often."

Keiko Oikawa is a Japanese food/lifestyle photographer based in the UK. Her award-winning blog, Nordljus, documents her experiences, from cooking and seasonal ingredients to travel, artisan producers, and photography assignments.

LAIA GARCIA

Blog: Geometric Sleep
http://www.geometricsleep.com

"Basically the only advice I can give someone who's just starting their blog is to completely ignore everything else that is out there and write and post about things that they are truly passionate about (whether good or bad). My blog is basically a journal of sorts and I guess people identify with my voice and aesthetic and that's how I've gotten some press, but it's not something I am after. I think, especially now that there are so many blogs out there, people are into finding something authentic, which I think is still the most important thing when creating anything at all."

Laia Garcia is a New York City-based fashion writer and stylist whose blog, Geometric Sleep, regularly appears on lists of top style blogs. When I asked if she had some advice for a new blogger this was her uncompromisingly honest answer.

BOWIE STYLE

Blog: Print & Pattern

http://printpattern.blogspot.com

"Back in 2005 I was working as an in-house textile designer who found there was a shift happening from using magazines to make trendboards towards searching for digital images on the internet. I discovered several American blogs that featured some pattern design, but there didn't seem to be any sites solely dedicated to her particular genre. So I decided to start my own under a pseudonym (based on a book about my hero David Bowie), and began to share my own observations. Since then it has really grown in readership and, amazingly, resulted in my own magazine column and several book contracts, after I was contacted by a publisher who had spotted Print & Pattern on the web."

Bowiestyle is the pseudonym of British designer and author Marie Perkins who started the Print & Pattern blog in 2006.

PETE BARNETT

Blog: The Strange Attractor

http://thestrangeattractor.net

"Everyone knows the more you put in to something the more you get out. It was fascinating how true this correlation was while trying to grow TSA. Some weeks my energy level would plateau, and so too would our traffic. The next week I would spend hours searching for new artists and uncovering fascinating creative work. Traffic would inevitably grow.

One day it dawned on me to invite other creatives to join. I went through old blog posts and generated a list of about sixteen exceptional artists. I was expecting to hear back from maybe a couple. To my utter surprise I heard back from nearly everyone and was able to bring on board twelve. This was a major turning point for us as the true community spirit of TSA took hold."

Pete Barnett started The Strange Attractor (TSA) in 2008, with the aim of sharing exceptional art from around the world.

NANCY CLAEYS

Blog: A Rural Journal

http://www.aruraljournal.com

"Right from the start I've published a blog post every day, and have made it a point to visit every blogger who has visited me and left a comment. It's work and it takes time, but I believe that has been a big reason behind my blogging success. My top tips? 1: Keep your blog posts simple, when appropriate. Just because it's an ordinary topic to you, doesn't mean it isn't interesting to someone else. Some of my most popular posts have been about the simplest concepts. 2: Post positive thoughts 99% of the time. Comments too. Don't criticize other bloggers in posts or comments. Don't constantly gripe about your life, spouse, kids, work. People read blogs to escape this stuff. Don't you? 3: Always admit when you are wrong. Your readers will appreciate and respect honesty."

Nancy Claeys has been blogging since 2007. In August 2010 she started A Rural Journal, which attracts a large, engaged audience.

NICHE BLOG COMMUNITIES

Whatever the subject of your blog, you are never alone. One way to draw energy and inspiration, make blogging buddies, and gain exposure for your blog is to join a niche community. Once you find a niche community or two, the blogosphere will seem a much more manageable space. Here are a few ideas to start you off, but I'm sure you will find more.

Photography

Photography blog communities often revolve around particular genres (fashion, weddings, food, etc.); platforms and tools (blog hosts, Photoshop, etc.); and top photographers. A few examples:

Light Stalking (http://www.lightstalking.com)
A site about beautiful photography and the people who make it. Says founder Rob Wood: "We want to give people a natural place to share their ideas on photography. As the community becomes more and more involved, the project takes on a life of its own."

Chase Jarvis (http://blog.chasejarvis.com/blog)
International photographer Chase Jarvis and his team blog about everything and anything to do with photography. Not strictly speaking a community, but certainly a hub of discussion for photographers. (As an example, a post entitled "Preset Photo Adjustments: Instant Gold or Drab Repetition?" attracted 117 comments in a couple of days.)

Pixyblog (http://www.pixyblog.com)
This is a photoblog hosting platform with add-ons such as "featured photographer" and a support wiki. Good example of a "specialist" blog host.

Art, crafts & design

CraftPlace (http://www.craftplace.org)
Crafters can have their blogs featured, connect and collaborate with others, and join or start discussions. Hosted by the Craft & Hobby Association of the USA.

Etsy Vintage Team (http://etsyvintage.blogspot.com)
This is an example of a niche "community within a community." All members of the Etsy Vintage Team (EVT) have been given a "stamp of approval" as trustworthy, reliable sellers on Etsy. They also serve as a resource for each other, sharing information and ideas on the EVT Blog.

Divaani Blogit (http://www.divaaniblogit.fi)
Finland has over 2,000 interior design blogs, and they are brought together in this community blog hosted by the publisher of Finnish magazine *Divaani*. The idea of the blog is to "create a visual and interactive community that promotes and develops Finnish design and home decorating culture."

Fashion

Chictopia (http://www.chictopia.com)
A big favorite with fashion bloggers and having over 100,000 registered users, Chictopia is a magazine, a resource, and a community, based around the idea of "what looks good on you?"

Independent Fashion Bloggers (http://heartifb.com)
A busy community founded in 2007 with the aim of helping fashion bloggers share experiences, promote their work, and create better blogs. A "weekly round up" offers twenty members the chance to see one of their blog posts featured prominently on the site.

Food

TasteSpotting (http://www.tastespotting.com)
A site that describes itself as a "highly visual potluck . . . a collection of eye-catching images that link to something deliciously interesting on the other side." Submissions are reviewed by an editorial board.

Foodista (http://www.foodista.com)
Aiming to create the world's largest food encyclopedia, Foodista encourage community contributions, wiki-style editing, and use of blogger tools for co-promotion.

FoodBlogs (http://www.foodblogs.com)
Although more of an aggregator or directory than a community, FoodBlogs ranks well in searches and has features such as the ability to "vote" for popular blog posts, rather like a social bookmarking site. It's free to join, and owned by the same company as MommyBlogs.

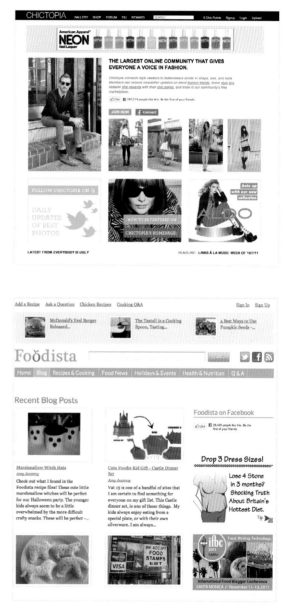

WHERE TO GO FOR MORE

There are many, many great resources on the web for the aspiring blogger. Here are just a few that I personally recommend. Not everyone agrees with everyone else about what constitutes blogging wisdom, and there's no "one way"–we're all learning as we go along–but these guys are all considered to be pretty much experts. Good luck, and may your blogging journey be everything you want it to be!

ProBlogger (http://www.problogger.net)
Darren Rowse first came across blogging in 2002 and was hooked. He started ProBlogger in 2004, a site "dedicated to helping other bloggers learn the skills of blogging, share their own experiences, and promote the blogging medium." ProBlogger now houses more than 3,500 articles, tips, tutorials, and case studies– well worth subscribing to.

Chris Brogan (http://www.chrisbrogan.com)
Chris Brogan is a consultant and speaker on the future of business communications, as well as being a *New York Times* bestselling co-author of *Trust Agents* and a featured monthly columnist at *Entrepreneur Magazine*. His blog is in the top five of the *Advertising Age* Power150. Always original and always relevant, he's not afraid to "think aloud" on his blog, which is full of down-to-earth blogging advice.

CopyBlogger (http://www.copyblogger.com)
Brian Clark founded CopyBlogger in 2006 and has been named on numerous "top blogs" lists. UK national paper *The Guardian* put CopyBlogger in their "World's 50 most powerful blogs" and Technorati, *Business Week*, and *Advertising Age* have all rated it as a top marketing blog. CopyBlogger covers all aspects of creating original blog content that will generate more traffic, links, subscribers, and profits.

Seth's Blog (http://sethgodin.typepad.com)
Bestselling author, speaker, and marketing guru Seth Godin's daily blog is famous for its bite-sized posts and unique style. Don't be put off by how bare it looks—Seth tends not to use images or allow comments, which goes against all the blogging "received wisdom"—but hey! He's Seth Godin, and just about everything he produces is thought-provoking and authentic.

Successful Blog (http://www.successful-blog.com)
This is the blog of social web strategist, community builder, and connector Liz Strauss. She has over 20 years' of experience in print, software, and online publishing. Liz's blog has won numerous awards and notable mentions. Check out her "new blogger" page—it contains an incredible amount of useful information and links for anyone starting out in blogging.

INDEX

NORTHBROOK COLLEGE SUSSEX
LEARNING RESOURCE CENTRE
LIBRARY

ACKNOWLEDGMENTS

I would like to thank the following people for all their help, support, and advice: my research assistants on this project Lucy Waters and Sue McKinney, Charlotte Howard of Fox & Howard Literary Agency, Ellie Wilson and Nick Jones of Ilex Press, Emma Shackleton, Rachel Carter, Sam McArthur, Andy White, and my ever-supportive husband Nick Houghton.

And of course, a huge thank you to all the lovely bloggers featured in the book, for sharing your expertise, and for responding patiently to all my emails.